Creating a successful
fashion collection

Creating a successful
fashion collection

Steven Faerm

BARRON'S

First edition for North America published in 2012 by
Barron's Educational Series, Inc.

A QUARTO BOOK

All inquiries should be addressed to:
Barron's Educational Series, Inc.
250 Wireless Boulevard
Hauppauge, New York 11788
www.barronseduc.com
ISBN: 978-0-7641-4732-6

Library of Congress Control No.: 2011937051

QUAR.WCFD

Conceived, designed, and produced by
Quarto Publishing plc
The Old Brewery
6 Blundell Street
London
N7 9BH

Senior editor Katie Crous
Copy editor Caroline West
Art director Caroline Guest
Art editor Joanna Bettles
Designer Karin Skånberg
Picture research Sarah Bell
Photographer Michael DeVito
Proofreader Karolin Thomas
Indexer Helen Snaith

Creative director Moira Clinch
Publisher Paul Carslake

Color separation by PICA Digital Pte Ltd., Singapore
Printed in Singapore by Star Standard Pte Ltd.

10 9 8 7 6 5 4 3 2 1

Contents

Continued overleaf ▶

EMMETT THE CRAZY SCIENTIST.

Introduction

There is a myriad of opportunities in the fashion world, but the industry is more competitive than ever. You will need to know how to present yourself professionally to be successful, making sure that you are noticed in a sea of budding talent.

There is an abundance of design talent today. Fashion weeks are held in most major international cities, from Paris to Rio de Janeiro. Schools are witnessing dramatic spikes in enrollment and are graduating students to work in both international industries and more locally. Because of our increasing awareness of aesthetics, there is an unprecedented demand for design talent. However, with fashion design programs producing countless graduates each year, as well as new study programs being created in every corner of the world, how can graduates outshine the competition?

The development of a portfolio that flaunts your talents, a collection that marks your entry into the profession, a résumé that articulates your abilities, and mastering the interview are just some of the topics examined in this book. There are certain crucial skills and attributes that all successful design leaders should display. The ones described here are considered essential in today's hyper-competitive world of fashion design.

1 Flaunt your talent, passion, and drive

Few potential designers have the insatiable passion that is expected by the fashion industry. Being a designer is a lifestyle choice, often marked by long hours and an all-consuming devotion to perfection. Some might describe this as "obsession," whereas others may advise that "if you don't eat, sleep, and breathe fashion, then choose another career." Drive shows in your work and personality; it conveys your level of dedication to being a designer.

2 Exhibit high levels of professionalism

Given the high number of graduates that interviewers have to choose from, it's a given that you must be supremely professional in everything you do. Everyone you meet in life is interviewing you. Strong organizational skills are imperative in today's multitasking world. As you develop your graduate portfolio, croquis book, and collection, remember that you are giving a visual representation of yourself. What you show speaks volumes about how you will perform on the job for which you are being interviewed.

3 Display a team-player attitude

Being able to work harmoniously with others is critical to your professional success. Employers are far more likely to hire a candidate who adds positively to their team than the more talented candidate who has a challenging personality. Team members who support one another, bond professionally, and enjoy working together will always outperform members of a team who may be more talented, yet clash with one another. Being a part of the company's culture is also essential.

4 Show a high degree of self-awareness

A true hallmark of successful people is their ability to understand who they are and what they want from life. When you are happy and fulfilled, you perform better, don't view work as "work," and have the highest level of motivation. Understand that not every design room is for everyone and that each has its own unique culture; it may take several places of employment before you find the perfect match.

About this book

This book outlines the key attributes and exemplary work employers are looking for. You should leave college with a final collection and graduate portfolio—your "debut" into the professional world—and if you're already there, this book will help you stand out from the crowd.

CHAPTER 1: BUILDING YOUR GRADUATE COLLECTION
The first portion of this book explores the final collection. Starting with the development of a conceptual foundation on which to build through customer identification and the research process, this section then looks at design and realization. The design process provides an overview for the development of the collection, including fabrication, the croquis book, trial "drapes," and a merchandising plan. The section concludes with an explanation of the logistical elements required to produce the collection, as well as those that will strengthen the final presentation.

Useful snippets of information are pulled out for easy reference

Key learning targets are given at the start of each unit

Real, exemplary design work, such as these croquis book pages, features throughout

The checklists for each main unit guide you to critically evaluate your own work

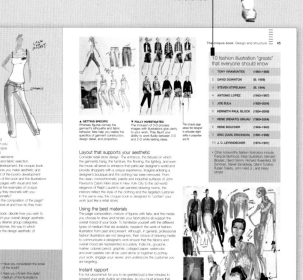

CHAPTER 2: MAXIMIZING YOUR PORTFOLIO

The second chapter examines the portfolio and other forms of design collateral. The portfolio's organization, the hallmarks of a successful layout, the benefits of online exposure, how to focus and target your work, and what to consider when developing your work for specific markets are all discussed.

Golden rules and insider tips are summarized and explained

Learn how to target your portfolio successfully to a specific market

Real-life portfolio pages illustrate strategic points in the design process

Runway shots of completed student work and professional designers' pieces display the end result

Full figure drawings feature alongside sketches and flats, showing the development of the collection

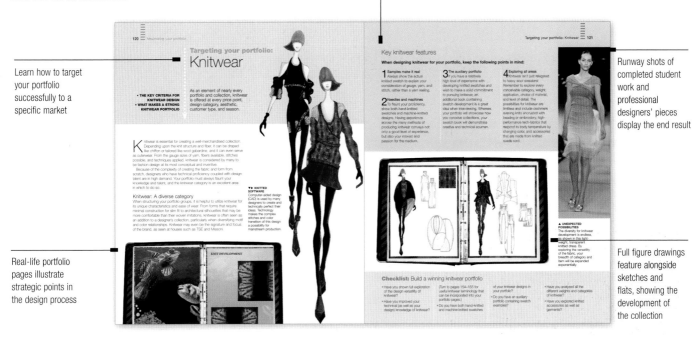

CHAPTER 3: GOING PROFESSIONAL

The book concludes with a discussion of the essential ingredients for succeeding in today's competitive industry. Transitioning from the classroom to the design room, how to succeed at interviews, the attributes of in-demand applicants, and a listing of careers within the industry provide a deeper understanding for portfolio development and what professionals are seeking.

Practical, realistic guides to finding, securing, and excelling in a career in fashion design

Essential dos and don'ts from inside the industry

A list of questions you can ask yourself to check that you are performing at your best and that you make the most of every opportunity

Where is fashion headed?

The industry's traditional systems are constantly being rethought and questioned by designers and graduates who must respond to, and act as agents of, change.

▶ **EXTREME IDENTITY**
In today's saturated market, designers must offer highly original and creative solutions to stand out. The dramatic proportions and technological fabrication give this coat an indelible impression of the designer's creative vision.

◀▲ **EMOTIONAL CONNECTION**
In today's oversaturated market, a strong conceptual framework, such as that of conjoined twins, as seen here, gives a collection personal meaning and enhances the emotional attachment of the customer to your aesthetic world. Innovative details surpass mere "product."

The speed of change that global communities are undergoing is unprecedented. With the rise in urban development, increased rates of consumption, shifts in cultural behavior, advances in technology, improved access to information, and many other factors driving us forward, the world has to adjust as never before. The fashion industry is no different. With so much change occurring in the fashion industry, how will the role of the future fashion designer evolve? How will education respond in order to prepare successful graduates to meet these demands, while also implementing more effective modes of operation?

The forces that are directing the future of the fashion design industry will, in turn, influence how future designers are educated. No longer strictly a vocation, the fashion design profession will become a more academic and theory-driven field in which designers will be expected to innovate existing systems, while also proposing new speculations. Consumers will be enticed through innovation and unexpected design. Items will contain a deeper level of narrative for the consumer to enjoy and connect with emotionally. Designers will be required to consider the impact their products make on the planet, as consumers become more aware of environmental issues and thus demand more environmentally friendly products.

Changing work patterns and locations

From New York's iconic 7th Avenue to Milan's knitwear facilities, the historic centers of fashion production are now distancing themselves from the design rooms, which are still located in fashion capitals such as New York, Paris, and Milan. What were once shared spaces of design and production are now being replaced by communication through email and Skype. Although designers were once adjacent to their sample rooms and performed draping and pattern-making alongside their technicians, their involvement in these hands-on stages is lessening. Given these facts, how many technical skills will design students need to master?

▶ **FASHIONABLE MASSES**
The widespread interest and demand for affordable designer fashion is evidenced by retailers partnering with exclusive designers, such as the H&M collaboration with Stella McCartney. What was once available to the minority can now be enjoyed by the majority.

Increasing demand from sophisticated consumers

The world of fashion design has exploded within the past two decades. What was once the concern of an elite few has now turned designers such as Louis Vuitton and Marc Jacobs into household names. As seen with such design partnerships as Karl Lagerfeld, Comme des Garçons, Lanvin, and Viktor and Rolf for H&M; Vera Wang for Kohl's; and Isaac Mizrahi and Liberty of London for Target, today's consumer gravitates toward products that were once considered for the minority.

This "passion for fashion" has created an unprecedented demand for new products, and the world's garment manufacturers have responded by overwhelming its audiences with choices. With such a high quantity and diversity of clothing on offer today, what is considered "good" design? Has this constant exposure changed our feelings toward fashion design? Has continuous demand for new products added to the skills that fashion designers must now have?

▼ **CHANGING LANDSCAPES**
The divide between the design room and production centers is widening. With over 90 percent of American fashion being made overseas, rather than in centers such as Manhattan's Garment District as has been in the past, there is bound to be an impact on the future of fashion education and the changing role of the designer.

▶ **GLOBAL BY NAME**
Marc Jacobs' brand has become a household name, and this reflects our culture's intense focus on, and demand for, top design. As more designers flood the market to meet these demands, different types of creativity will emerge in order to sustain a brand's unique identity.

▶ CLOTHING THAT CARES
Launched in 2005 by Bono's wife, Ali Hewson, Edun aims to promote fair business practices in developing nations while sustaining local communities.

Technology has served as the primary agent of this change: with the advent of design-themed television programs and the accessibility of information via the Internet, the world's populations have been raised on, and educated by, sophisticated design. With such advanced tastes and demand for well-designed products, how can future designers stand out from other designers?

The impact of celebrity designers

Like most professions, the once-rarified world of the fashion designer was led by creative individuals who mastered the craft through years of schooling and apprenticeships. Yves Saint Laurent worked under Christian Dior, Jean-Paul Gaultier under Pierre

Cardin, Alber Elbaz under Geoffrey Beene, and Nicolas Ghesquiere under Jean-Paul Gaultier. A radical shift was seen when talented young designers were catapulted into fashion stardom. Labels such as Proenza Schouler, Ohne Titel, and Vena Cava were all launched by students within their first few years of graduation, and consumers were quick to respond to their fresh ideas. Alongside this new talent, the "designer-by-name" phenomenon came into the fashion industry. Now, any famous name can become a designer, regardless of their actual involvement in the process. Jessica Simpson, Jennifer Lopez, Justin Timberlake, the Olsen twins, and a host of others have all created brands based on their pop-culture fame. This has prompted many in the industry to ask, "What does being a 'designer' mean today?"

◀ CELEBRITY ADAPTATIONS
Following their high-priced collection "The Row," the Olsen twins debuted the juniors line "Olsenboye" with JC Penney in 2010. Designers typically debut a diffusion line that is more affordable once they establish their primary line.

The environment and sustainability

Our world is in a crisis. Events such as chemical spills in sensitive ecosystems, deforestation, global warming, and toxic emissions into the atmosphere as a result of production facilities and landfills that have reached breaking point are prompting the world's communities to examine their consumption habits. How much do we really need? How do our actions impact on the planet in both the short- and long-term? How can we make better choices? How do we define "need" and "desire"? How can new practices be developed that sustain the environment and local communities?

◀ ADDRESSING CONCERNS
Sustainability has become a manifesto for some designers who provide the consumer with deeper levels of social consciousness. Junkie Styling is one such brand that reconfigures discarded garments into unique pieces, without sacrificing innovative design.

▼ MESSAGES AND MEANING
Today's sophisticated consumer wishes to learn about a collection's development in order to connect to the product. The hand movements of traditional Thai massage give this collection an unmistakable hallmark, and its wearer a unique experience.

NANAE TAKATA

The 10 hallmarks of
A successful collection

The defining hallmarks of a successful collection encompass practical, artistic, and conceptual considerations. When all these aspects support one another, the collection is rich in content and context, and it also displays a professional confidence.

▶ DEFINING YOUR MUSE
Brands succeed due to their acute sensitivity toward their targeted customer or muse. Hussein Chalayan often researches academic theories when constructing his collections in order to appeal to consumers who demand deeper levels of meaning in the clothing they wear.

◀ OSCAR DE LA RENTA
The romantic world of Oscar de la Renta is captured in this look. Designers must avoid being "everything to everyone" in order to capture a specific demographic that aspires to be a part of their fashion fantasy.

1 Advances fashion forward
With every collection, an evolution of style is suggested by the designer. How consumers approach fashion and what they demand from design changes rapidly. However, when viewed through a historical lens, successful design leads this evolution. It takes risks and calls for the designer to have a remarkable intuition, as the collections proposed are for months (if not years) ahead of retail.

2 Shows mastery of execution
When fabrication, silhouette, and construction are successfully synthesized, fashion design rises to the professional level. Like a painter choosing a canvas scale and medium, a designer chooses specific fabrication, cut, scale, and finishing techniques to communicate the collection's statement.

3 Has a clearly articulated customer/muse
Fashion must be aspirational. From the elite worlds of Oscar de la Renta (far left) and Ralph Lauren to the intelligence of Jil Sander and Prada and the cerebral concepts of Hussein Chalayan (left) and Viktor and Rolf, your customer must aspire to be a part of your fantasy world. What entices a customer to choose one designer's black suit over another? Designers are always aware of creating lifestyles in which their audience wishes to participate.

4 Addresses a lifestyle
Who are your customers? What are their needs? What kind of life do they lead? Donna Karan began her label because of the fashion demands of the rising female workforce of the 1980s. Karan's own professional life inspired her to create a wardrobe of "essentials" that took a woman through the working week (right). By understanding your customers' needs in this way, you can strategically formulate collections with merchandising, fabrications, colors, and silhouettes.

5 Is visionary
Designers shape, refine, and question the world that they construct. Like the foundation of a building, the designer's vision serves as a touchstone on which to construct each consecutive collection.

▲ CHANGING NEEDS
Donna Karan found success when she created her "7 Easy Pieces," which gave the newly emerging 1980s corporate woman key items for an essential wardrobe.

Fashion is always "extreme," whether it is extreme minimalism, as often seen with Jil Sander, or extreme narrative, as utilized by Alexander McQueen. Design must always be confident and unadulterated in order to maintain identity.

9 Is innovative

The ability to innovate design within the context of what is traditionally accepted can earn your work great recognition. Consider the revolution that occurred when Yves Saint Laurent used utilitarian clothing, such as the peacoat, in a couture collection. As we advance forward, innovation is being seen in textile development, technology embedded in clothing—such as Zegna's solar-powered jacket for recharging iPods and cellphones—and production methods.

6 Shows that fashion is extreme

Fashion is never safe and always displays a level of extremity, depending on how that designer defines "extreme." From the minimalism of Jil Sander (above left) to the pattern combinations of Oilily and Etro, from the silhouettes and proportions of Yohji Yamamoto and Lanvin to the historicism of the late Alexander McQueen (above right), fashion design displays an unadulterated view of a unique world proposed by the designer.

10 Builds momentum and provides narration

An essential element in any runway show is the order in which the theme is presented. For some designers, defined color palettes that form individual groups offer small, digestible capsules. Others build a narrative, starting with conventional silhouettes and finishing with a crescendo that reflects a fantasy world of extremes, as was often seen in the work of Alexander McQueen. Another practice is to have levels of extremity filtered throughout a collection. Whichever format is used, it is essential to retain an element of surprise and cohesion throughout.

7 Is non-referential

The designer's role is to form a unique artistic "voice." A designer must stand apart from other contemporary or historic designers, and manipulate inspiration into highly personal collections. This is particularly important when forming a new label. In order to garner press and customer appeal, you must offer a unique vision.

▼ THE BODY AS BAROMETER
Fashion reflects our current and future world. The rectangular, youthful silhouettes of the 1920s and 1960s reflected the dominant youth culture following the wasp-waisted silhouettes of the previous decade.

8 Reflects and predicts our cultural climate

Designers have a sixth sense that allows them to predict consumer behavior and comment on our evolving world. Serving as a cultural barometer ensures that customers' needs are addressed. When you view historical fashion, what do the colors, silhouettes, and fabrics say about the society's attitudes? How did women wish to feel and/or how did society impose its views on them? Consider the similarities in fashion during the 1920s and the mod 1960s (right).

Building your graduate collection

How does the graduate collection show evidence of everything that you've learned? How can the work be used to convey your professional goals? How can the collection provide the first mark on your professional timeline? Entering the design process strategically will ensure your collection best serves your intended career trajectory.

For most students the graduate collection is their first foray into a body of work that is not only on a grand scale, but also of great importance. As the culmination of all that has been learned during the previous academic years, your collection provides you with an opportunity to execute a grouping of "looks" from start to finish. As the first mark on your professional timeline, it is truly a debut into the professional world and will be judged as such in terms of both design and execution.

This chapter guides you through the stages involved in creating your collection, including the initial inspiration, an extensive research process, fabric development and research, a rigorous sketching process where ideas are developed and tested, draping and pattern-making for creating muslin prototypes, and the execution of final samples. These clear stages will test not only your knowledge and talent, but also your dedication to becoming a fashion designer. It is a true initiation into the fashion design process.

The academic year

- **LEARN WHAT WILL HAPPEN AT EACH STAGE OF THE COURSE**
- **LEARN HOW TO PRESENT YOURSELF AND YOUR WORK PROFESSIONALLY**

When developing your final collection, you will need to follow a strict schedule to ensure that the work is completed successfully and on time. The process is rigorous, and you will be expected to act professionally throughout.

The fall semester: Concepts and muslin prototypes

◄ THEMATIC VARIATIONS
Only by developing variations can a designer discover the best possibilities and solutions. This designer has sketched varieties of construction detail and print placement, which are framed by a recurring silhouette to provide focus.

Weeks 1 to 3: *Research and croquis development*
Perform extensive research, fabric swatching, fabric manipulations and treatments, and croquis 100 to 150 sketches.

Week 3: *Final edits presented*
Edit down to the looks that will become the collection. These final sketches should be regarded only as a foundation from which to begin the 3-D process. As you develop muslin prototypes, develop and refine ideas while further researching and perfecting fabric proposals.

Week 4: *Look 1 due*
You should be developing Look 1 during weeks 1 to 4. This could include the drafting of a basic pant or jacket that will then be modified between weeks 3 and 4.

Week 6: *Look 2 due*

Week 8: *Look 3 due*

Week 10: *Look 4 due*
At this stage, review the collection, the relationships between the looks, and how the remaining looks will be realized. Have ideas evolved and improved? Do the remaining looks need to be reconsidered because of any changes? How has the original fabric story altered? Have changes affected the intended mood and customer?

Week 12: *Look 5 due*

Week 14: *Look 6 due*

Week 15: *Final review of all looks*
Looks are assessed for the overall collection's mood, cohesion, proportion, fabrication, fabric samples, and design decisions. You will cut your first garment in final fabric during this week.

January break
During this month, devote your time to elements for which you do not need faculty guidance. Fabric dyeing, beading, screen printing, basic garment construction, and other simple details are all worked on. When you return to school in February, you will focus on finishing the work that requires guidance.

The process in which a collection is developed is similar on all major fashion design courses. The fall semester will be devoted to developing the collection's foundation through research, fabric development and experimentation, croquis sketching, and muslin prototypes. After the finalization of muslin prototypes through an analysis of fit, proportion, and the collection's context, fabrications are finalized and final samples are produced. During the winter break, all fabric treatments are produced along with other less challenging aspects of the collection. When you return for the spring semester, you will finish the collection with the aid of your faculty. The following breakdown of a typical academic year outlines the goals you will need to achieve at each stage.

▲ FINISHING ALLOWANCES
When sewing your final samples, allow for generous seam allowances. This will enable you to adjust proportion for aesthetic preferences in both width and length when viewing the work on a live, moving model.

The spring semester: Final fabrication

Week 1: **Look 1 due**

Week 3: **Look 2 due**

Week 5: **Look 3 due**
Students begin to rehearse their presentations with faculty for the collection week.

Week 7: **Look 4 due**

Week 9: **Look 5 due**

Week 11: **Look 6 due; final review with faculty before collection review**

Week 12: **Presentation rehearsals**
Students work with faculty on how to present their work through the description of the inspiration and a showing of garments.

Week 13: **Collection presentations**

Week 14: **The fashion show**

Week 15: **Final portfolio presentations**

Collection presentations

As a future fashion designer, it is essential to learn the art of presenting your work professionally. Like an actor, your speech, body language, energy, and confidence must engage your audience. You must believe strongly in your work so that others will follow.

At the end of the year, a jury will view your work and presentation. Designers, faculty, fashion industry professionals, and others qualified to analyze design will attend. Each student presents his or her collection, speaking about the collection and answering any questions. Depending on those present, your review may be a valuable opportunity to show your work to a fashion leader and gain insightful feedback on how to succeed in your future career.

Checklist: An effective thesis presentation

- Are you adhering to a strict work schedule?
- Have you developed a strong foundation for the collection through research?

- Has the croquis sketching been conducted thoroughly?
- Have the muslin prototypes been considered within the collection's context?

- Have all fabric treatments been produced in the winter break?
- Are you confident that you can present your work in a professional manner?

- Will your presentation excite and engage your audience?
- Are you maximizing your opportunities with people who will be present?

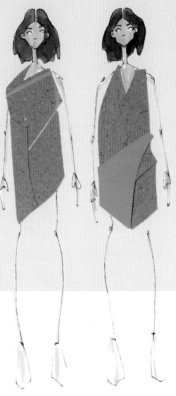

The collection:
Purpose and aims

- **USE THE COLLECTION TO FLAUNT YOUR STRENGTHS AND SKILLS**
- **USE THE COLLECTION AS A SPRINGBOARD TO COMMERCIAL SUCCESS**

The collection serves as the first mark on your professional timeline. It presents your vision as a designer to the industry and will evolve and strengthen over time.

During undergraduate design education, the various disciplines of fashion design are explored to give students a full understanding of the practice. This explanation of how different design problems are solved provides future designers with the ability to discover which areas they respond to most and which types of design they feel most inspired by. For example, students with highly colorful fabric stories often gravitate toward childrenswear, whereas those who enjoy the engineering and ergonomics of design often respond to accessory design.

By your final year, the years of experimentation with design will result in a body of work that depicts where you are heading professionally. The customer/muse you address, how you approach fashion design, and the vision you've cultivated will be presented in the form of a graduate portfolio and collection. Although this may seem daunting, it is merely the beginning of your creative self that will constantly evolve for decades to come. Like all great artists, your work can never stagnate if you are to address the shifting moods of your culture, as well as your own tastes.

▼ **CONCEPT INTO CLOTHING**
The design sketches provide clarity for building a collection. Fabrication, motif, and merchandising are all design elements that must be considered at this stage.

◀ **PROPORTION COLLAGE**
Using collaged paper can trigger silhouette, color placement, and even construction ideas.

Checklist: Developing your thesis

- Does your thesis collection convey your unique vision?
- Is your thesis an adequate reflection of your conceptual and technical abilities?

- Are you showcasing your real strengths and attributes?
- Does your thesis work take you out of your "skill set"?

- Have you fulfilled yourself creatively and created highly personal work?
- Are you continually reflecting on and exploring who you are as a designer?

- Is your thesis an adequate stepping-stone into the professional world?
- Will your collection ultimately allow you to start your own label?

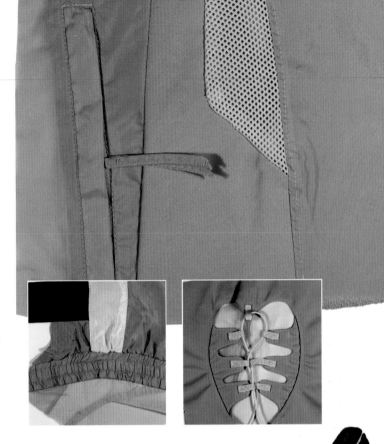

Demonstrating and flaunting your strengths

Like your graduate portfolio, your collection is a creative and emotional representation of you. It conveys your unique vision and much of what you believe in and are capable of doing, both conceptually and technically.

It is vital that you assess your skill level and work within it. A collection is not deemed more successful simply because of complicated construction or fabrics that require a professional technician. Always showcase your strengths, whether they are innovative silhouettes and seaming, or textile designs and fabric manipulations supported with simple garment silhouettes.

A foundation for your career

The collection and your ability to present your work professionally mark your formal entry into the professional world. Your collection should be viewed as a first step into the professional arena, where you will be judged as a young designer and not as a developing student. It is an essential ingredient in your search for a job and can even serve as the foundation for beginning your own label.

You should also regard your collection as the final project that you will execute as a student, and one that allows you to design strictly for yourself according to your own unadulterated vision. Relish this creative freedom and use your time to create work that is deeply personal and investigative.

Because of its scale, the collection should also be seen as an ongoing exploration of who you are as a designer. The connections you make between the collection and future projects will place the collection in a context that enables you to make informed decisions as you advance professionally. Allowing yourself to reflect on your development over time will strengthen your creative and professional goals for the future.

▲ CONVINCING SAMPLES
Articulating design concepts in fabric samples and treatments ensure that initial speculations will be successful. Actual fabrics (rather than muslin/calico) are required, along with all trims selected.

▼ THE FINAL COUNTDOWN
Editing occurs after the design process has been fully examined; it ensures successful merchandising. This collection avoids redundancy due to its variation of items, color relationships, and fabric weights.

The collection:
Key stages of development

To build your collection strategically, the steps of production must be mapped out, during which you are able to reflect on what has been done and anticipate the upcoming phases. Here is an overview of these phases, to keep you on track.

1 Inspiration and research

First decide what you want your collection to say to your audience, as well as what it should elicit visually. Is it slick, urban, and sculptural, or delicate, feminine, and charming? Is it aggressive, militant, and assertive, or seductive, billowy, and ethereal? Begin by listing adjectives, which will provide inspiration for color, fabric, and silhouette, and how the garments will move and feel on the body.

Although your selected words will provide the inspiration to kick-start your research, the time spent combing through books, the Internet, museums, libraries, and any other sources are likely to lead you to unexpected ideas. Let the research process guide you. It should be done thoughtfully, slowly, and critically, so that you may consider how one area of research can lead to the next deeper level or a different area altogether.

2 Using color for effect

Color, its scale, and the context of the surrounding colors must be evaluated closely to create the desired emotions. When viewing professional designers' work, consider how a similar color can be used with strikingly different results because of such factors as the palette's overall context. For example, a pale yellow in a palette of khakis and creams may read as a tonal variation, whereas the same yellow used with other primary colors would look bold and tropical. Similarly, how does color suggest a targeted market and aesthetic? Graphic and contrasting color combinations, commonly used in activewear, often feel young and less serious, while tonal combinations that elongate the figure, such as those from Rick Owens or Donna Karan, appear more sophisticated and mature.

◄ FLUID DESIGN PROCESS
Developing your skills between the 2-D and 3-D design processes is critical. By performing both activities simultaneously, you will understand and develop your design on a deeper level.

◄ COURTING COLORS
Red, white, and blue are used here by Marc Jacobs in a graphic and athletic application to underscore the customer's lifestyle and attitude.

◀ PRIMARY BEGINNINGS
Always begin with primary research, including visits to museums (such as the Guggenheim, pictured here) and galleries.

3 Selecting appropriate fabrics

Using your research and textual beginnings as a foundation, begin looking for fabrics that will underscore the previous frameworks. You may have already considered silhouettes and garment details that will be sketched, so select the fabric fibers, weaves, and weights that will be required as well. As discussed later in this book, fabric choices must be well merchandised in order to address a range of items and constructions. For example, a fabric palette composed of wovens and knits in identical weights does not make for an engaging and well-considered story.

Start by sketching the most extreme elements of the collection. By starting with these aspects, which are closely connected to your inspiration, you will gradually translate design elements into other proportions, fabrications, usages, levels of practicality, and so on. Remember, it is always easier to filter down a literal idea or extreme element than it is to take a banal design and create something compelling from it.

As you croquis each phase, you will extrapolate ideas from the previous sketch session to continue with, as well as create new ideas. After each phase, consider photocopying the croquis groups in black and white so that the garment forms remain the focus, rather than the color, and select the sketches that you wish to continue developing.

▲ BEYOND MUSLIN
When developing your prototypes, you must use an inexpensive fabric that is similar to the final fabric. Coating weights, sheers, and various knits may be considered in addition to the more typically used cotton muslin.

4 Using the croquis process

Previous thumbnail sketches may have provided a suggested mood or served as a reminder for details to incorporate, but it is only after the processes described above have taken place that you are ready to begin the collection's development.

5 Editing down to a six-figure narrative

When you have completed a large quantity of sketches, begin the editing process for the final six looks. What do you want your viewers to experience? Will the collection evolve into the most extreme representation of the inspiration? Or, will the collection gain its impact through color, texture, silhouette, or fabrication extremes as the looks are presented? By planning the narrative, you will be able to solve merchandising questions; choose appropriate silhouettes, colors, and fabrication; and address styling.

◀ VARIED IMPACT
The range of color, its context, and particular adjacencies must all be considered. What could read as a subtle tonal range, as seen here, could alter radically simply by reordering the swatch placements.

6 Using prototypes and final samples

Like a blueprint, your sketches and flats serve as a directive to realize the collection in 3-D. Although you have made highly critical decisions when editing the work in sketch form, these early stages should serve only as a grounding element. The draping and pattern-making process will enable you to discover better solutions of fit, drape, proportion, and overall construction. You may find that what was initially proposed in sketch form does not resonate with you once it is borne on the form.

7 Finalizing your collection

After muslin and pattern corrections through the fitting process on a live model have taken place, final samples in the selected fabrics are ready to be made. At this stage, all design decisions, fabric choices and treatments, knit swatches, and finishes should have been decided on. Note that it is important to use time in the classroom for the more challenging areas of the collection's execution so that you have access to your instructors if you need guidance. Your own time can be used for less challenging areas of construction and those areas that are slow and labor intensive, such as beading or other handwork.

Inspiration and research:
Defining your market

- **KEY QUESTIONS TO ASK WHEN IDENTIFYING YOUR TARGET CUSTOMER**
- **UNDERSTANDING WHAT TO INCLUDE IN YOUR COLLECTION**

Understanding your target customer is critical, and you will need to demonstrate this understanding to a future employer. Your customer profile may be refined over the years, but it is essential to identify your consumer in order to achieve success as a fashion designer.

Your target customer will be defined by two major sets of criteria: demographics and psychographics. Demographics include factors such as gender, age, income, marital status, and number of children. Psychographics include factors such as personal values, lifestyle, career choice, hobbies, and personality. Analyzing both the demographics and the psychographics of your target customer is critical to understanding who he or she is. In fact, it is as important, if not more so, that you understand who this "person" is, as it is to know the specific type of design you wish to produce. Despite the desire for a world of free aesthetic, the reality is that you don't have a career if you don't have customers. And you won't have customers if you don't know who they are and don't ensure that you design specifically for them.

Many people/companies make the mistake of believing that "my/our target market is everyone who likes X!" This is almost a guarantee of failure. You must specialize and hone your focus. Remember the adage: you can't be all things to all people!

Identifying current and future competition
Equally important as defining your customer is identifying and understanding your competitors. As a recent graduate, the competition may at first be other graduates who are looking for an initial position in the industry. Once you've been working in the

◀▲ DRAMATIC PERSONA
Extreme texture, silhouette, and attitude give this collection an identity that is bold and unique.

Checklist: Understanding your target customer

- Have you assessed your target customer from a demographic and psychographic point of view?
- Do you understand what your target customer really needs and desires?

- Is your collection aimed at your target customer, or is it a reflection of your own vision?
- Have you assessed both current and future competition?
- Are you in a strong position to develop your own brand for the future?

- Have you compiled a list of essential "must-haves" for your line?
- Have you considered the type of product you would like to be designing in two, three, and five years?

- Are you paying close attention to changes in your market and target customer?
- Is your future vision flexible enough to adapt to a changing reality?

◄ HYBRID RESEARCH
The process for discovering your market and muse might entail the combination of several researched areas. This designer has merged various images to create one illustrated character profile.

industry for several years and are looking to break out on your own, your competition will be other new designers who have emerged over the last eighteen months, as well as those who are off the radar and will emerge in the coming eighteen months. Consider:
• Who are they?
• What's their niche market?
• What sets them apart from their competition?
You stand a much better chance of developing a strong brand for yourself and defining your own market if you have no direct competition.

Knowing your product
Just as you need to understand your client, so too do you need to understand your product. Using the list of criteria you've produced while identifying your target customer, you can begin to develop a list of "must-haves" for your line. Does your target customer buy activewear made only from organic materials? If so, you need to factor these resources into the production of your product. Does your target client have a strong desire for designer price-point

▼ RUNWAY TO REALITY
Every collection must offer different levels of design intensity in order to address varying lifestyle, price points, and customer. By beginning the design process with the purest form of design, you will be able to filter these into more familiar silhouettes.

fashion, but also need clothing that can withstand the mess created by a toddler? If so, you need to factor in the importance of easy-to-clean, low-maintenance fabrics and construction.

Although you may not have your own line immediately after your schooling, you need to know what the product is that you're currently working on, as well as what it will be two, three, and five years down the line. Are you currently working on childrenswear but wish to design high-end men's sportswear? Then you need to develop a plan to move from your present focus to your goal. Are you currently working on women's sportswear for an internationally renowned designer, but wish to have your own collection launched within five years? If this is the case, then you need to develop a plan to achieve this.

Ensuring that your vision is viable

After you've explored your target customer and identified the competition, you need to review your conclusions and make sure your vision is viable. Does your "customer" actually exist? Are there enough "customers" to make your vision economically viable? Does your design vision differ enough from that of your competitors to ensure it will stand out? And, most importantly of all, is it the vision that you want?

Your vision is not a static, solid entity; it is a fluid, malleable concept and will change as a result of your experiences—both within and outside the fashion industry—as well as your observations of the market and its customers. It is critical that you remain committed to having your own vision, rather than a pre-existing, specific vision. You must remain committed to ensuring that your vision reflects reality and adapts as reality changes.

Points to consider
when evaluating your target customers

- **Know who they are**
  Where do they live? Urban vs. suburban vs. rural. Consider their gender, age range, marital status; do they have children?

- **Know their interests**
  Do they travel? If so, is this domestically and/or internationally? Are they sports fans? Do they prefer the opera?

- **Know what they do**
  Do they have paid work or spend their days doing unpaid work (i.e., banking vice president vs. chair of the Junior League)?

- **Know their spending habits**
  What is their discretionary spending, in terms of both percentage of total income and actual amount?

- **Know their needs/ demands**
  Is quality or price more important? Natural or synthetic fabrics?

- **Know what drives their purchasing choices**
  Understand needs vs. desires; buying for work vs. a single-use night on the town.

◀▲ OFFERING A FULL SPECTRUM
The manners in which you convey your audience extend well beyond the clothing offered. This group uses bold, playful colors and simple, iconic accessory shapes to suggest a customer's personality and clothing preferences.

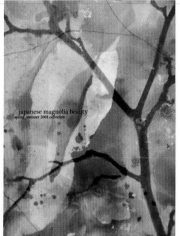

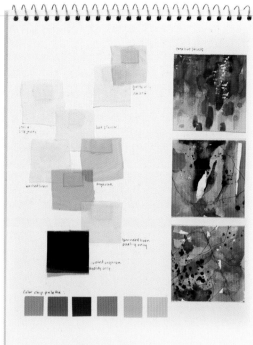

◄ SHARED QUALITIES

This collection maintains cohesion through the shared transparent quality in colors, fabrics, and print developments. By creating visual and tactile relationships, your collection will be focused to address one defined aesthetic.

▲ CREATING A MOOD

Like the entrance to a boutique, the mood board introduces your viewer to the attitude that will be conveyed in the clothing. Consider your mood pages as a piece of fine art that suggests rather than explains.

▼ SILHOUETTE SUPPORT

Designers are always cognizant of the emotional impact that textiles, colors, and prints can make in a collection. The sheer and billowy fabrics that are cut in loose, unconstructed shapes aesthetically support the soft watercolor prints in this resort collection.

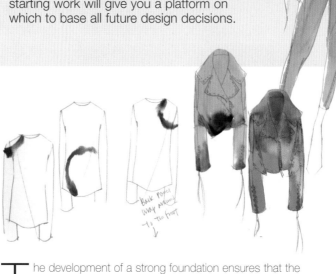

Inspiration and research:
Defining
the concept

• WHAT TO INCLUDE
IN A COLLECTION AND
HOW TO PRESENT IT
• HOW TO GIVE A
COLLECTION
INTELLECTUAL AND
EMOTIONAL MEANING

Planning the collection's message before starting work will give you a platform on which to base all future design decisions.

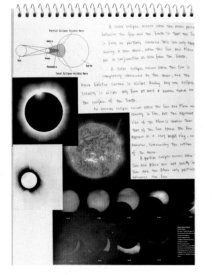

▲ EMBRACE SERENDIPITY
Enter the research process without predetermined outcomes through the use of images and notes. By entering the process openly, your research may lead you to new, unexpected, and exciting areas for greater design context.

The development of a strong foundation ensures that the visual narration, merchandising, and design cohesion of your collection will be more focused. How designers develop their collections is as diverse as fabric itself. Whereas some follow a strict rubric, others simply do as they wish and hope their audience will respond. For example, when Olivier Theyskens designed for Rochas, he avoided the rule of including trousers in the collections because of his own preferences. Other designers, particularly those at large design houses, receive mandates from a merchandising team on what must be designed and how many of each item.

The evolution of the presentation
As part of this foundation, designers consider how the "rhythm" of their collection will unfold. As looks are presented, a framework of

▲ DYEING FOR
INSPIRATION
A concept must be adapted in many techniques in order for a collection to convey depth. The discovery of circular tie-dye effects led to the application of ombré-dyeing and felting techniques, all derived from the same research.

Checklist: Creating visual narration

• Does the collection have a narrative-based foundation?

• Is there a clear transition from day wear to evening wear?

• Have you analyzed the key components of the collection?

• Does the introduction include tailored looks that feel controlled and business-like?

• Are the figures in the more casual central section segmented through color, texture, and silhouette?

• Does the finale exhibit the design extremes of the collection and include dramatic evening wear?

• Is there a creative depth and interpretation of inspiration?

• Does the collection challenge the existing design systems?

• Have you used contrasts to emphasize the collection's focus?

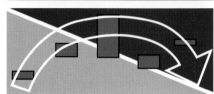

▲▶ METAPHORICAL ECLIPSE
The inspiration of an eclipse is used here both physically through garment detail and construction, and metaphorically through the presentation of color. Like the planetary event, light colors are gradually overshadowed by darks, whereas the orange accent color suggests the solar crescent shape, leading the eye in a semicircular direction.

category, color, fabrications, highly designed with simple pieces, and the transition from daytime to evening wear should provide the customer with a full wardrobe. Often beginning with tailored career sportswear, presentations evolve into casual sportswear that is more relaxed, followed by late-day and cocktail looks, and end with dramatic evening wear.

Although this is the format used by most designers, the sequencing of design to create cohesion and momentum will vary. For example, Alexander McQueen was renowned for historically rich collections that were often a synthesis of several themes. The visually progressive narrative led the viewer through a series of vignettes that often erupted into highly conceptual finales. Other designers, such as Miuccia Prada, use inspirations that are less overt and filter various design "intensities" throughout the presentation rather than relying on a grand, conceptual finale.

A supportive synthesis
The formation of your concept and inspiration will give breadth and depth to your collection's outcome. How deep a designer delves into these two parameters often reflects not only that designer's own creative development, but also the audience that demands such a narrative in order to appreciate the designer's work fully. Whereas some consider clothing to be an expression of intellectual and emotional meaning, other designers may be driven to produce work that is simply luxurious and aesthetically pleasing.

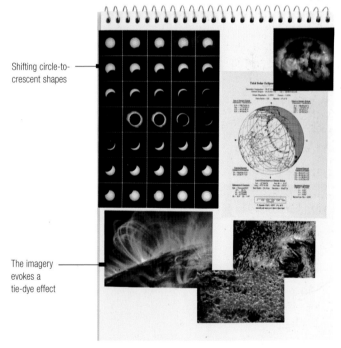

Shifting circle-to-crescent shapes

The imagery evokes a tie-dye effect

▲ MIND AND MATTER
Effective research creates design that incorporates physical and emotional elements. The dark/light transition suggests the solar eclipse, whereas the crescent shape created by overlapping planets is suggested through color placement. The sense of unease from these shifting planets is further exemplified through asymmetrical, shifted construction.

Analyzing the categories

When building your narrative, consider how the viewer's eye will move as the looks are presented through the different stages of the presentation:

1 Introduction Tailored looks shown at the beginning move the viewer's eye vertically through longer silhouettes, such as trench-coats and suits cut in matching fabrics. Because your eye moves in long, vertical gestures, the outfits feel controlled and pulled together, which is ideal for career sportswear.

2 Central section During the middle of the presentation, garments are designed to move the eye horizontally by segmenting the figure through color, texture, and silhouette. This section's more complicated design relationships allow for more item-driven pieces, which make the section feel more casual. This section often displays a more overt usage of theme and inspiration after the collection's less intense introduction.

3 Finale The collection's finale is to provide the audience with the exclamation mark of the collection's theme or the fantasy of evening wear. Often employing unique silhouettes, fabrics, and treatments, the finale exhibits the theme in its extremity (as is often seen in Hussein Chalayan's presentations) or as a continuation of the primary design motifs, as with Calvin Klein and Donna Karan.

Emphasizing the focus

How concepts are conceived and utilized often depends upon the types of contrasts that exist. For example, in order to convey darkness, an artist must use a small quantity of light. Similarly, for a designer to underscore a collection's emphasis of soft drapery, a portion of construction must be used. When such contrasts are used in this "yin-and-yang" format, an inspiration can be chosen that will support the design theories.

The designer's initials create a circular logo that references her inspiration

Core colors allow for a light-to-dark transition

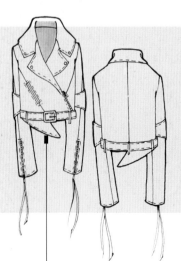

Rounded shapes move the eye and are reminiscent of the moon's crescent shape

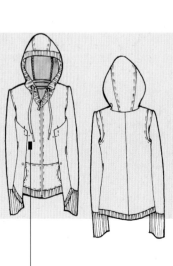

Inspired by the moving planets, panel construction shifts asymmetrically

▲ PREPPY/HIPPIE
When researching iconic lifestyles, examine how they can be conveyed through such physical means as color, fabric, silhouette, and details, in addition to how the core values of the groups may provide such design criteria as garment construction and usage.

▲ MACRO/MICRO
Examining the overall form, aesthetic, color palette, and mood of an interior space or building's exterior, along with the subject's minute details, will provide your collection with cohesive design criteria.

COMMONLY USED CONCEPTS	SUGGESTED INSPIRATION PAIRINGS
ORGANIC/LINEAR	ART MOVEMENTS: ART NOUVEAU/ART DECO
CONFORM/REBEL	POLITICAL OPPOSITES: PREPPY/HIPPIE
CONSTRUCTED/DECONSTRUCTED	ICONIC ARCHITECTURE: THE BAUHAUS SCHOOL/THE POMPIDOU CENTER
LUXURY/UTILITARIAN	MARIE ANTOINETTE'S ENVIRONMENTS: CENTER VERSAILLES/THE HAMLET
MASCULINE/FEMININE (E.G., HISTORICAL, CULTURAL)	JAPANESE HISTORICAL COSTUME: SAMURAI ARMOR/THE KIMONO
CLASSIC/AVANT-GARDE	FASHION HISTORY: ICONIC AMERICAN SPORTSWEAR/DECONSTRUCTION
INTERNAL/EXTERNAL	THE BIOLOGICAL STRUCTURE OF A FLOWER/THE GREENHOUSE
MACRO/MICRO	A CATHEDRAL'S VESTIBULE/SPECIFIC FORMS AND DETAILS WITHIN
LOCAL/FOREIGN	HOW DOES THIS REFLECT YOUR OWN ENVIRONMENT?

ART NOUVEAU/ART DECO
Effective thematic juxtapositions often begin with an overlying narrative arc. Selecting contrasting art movements will give you a particular framework from which to develop your design process.

Inspiration and research:
Building the research

- **WHY RESEARCH IS SO IMPORTANT TO THE CREATIVE PROCESS**
- **USING INSPIRATION BOOKS TO RECORD CREATIVE RESEARCH**

As the most critical foundation for developing your collection, the results of your research should provide you with a seemingly limitless stream of ideas.

By acquiring layers of inspiration that relate to one another, you will develop a collection that is richer in concept and design references. There are three main parts to the research process:

1 Mapping ideas The initial stages allow you to explore, play, and investigate specific areas of inspiration, while also coming across others serendipitously. Brainstorming by writing words on paper and linking them by association will help to get you thinking and will highlight any common themes.

◀ 1 MIND MAP
A mind map provides an essential foundation for defining your collection's direction. Adjectives will offer a rich reference from which all design criteria will develop, including mood, attitude, colors, fabrics, and silhouettes.

Checklist: The search for inspiration

- Have you identified your muse (i.e., the person you are designing for)?
- Does your research cover the four pillars (mood, color, silhouette, and detail)?

- Have you researched the original source of your inspiration?
- Have you taken both emotional and physical triggers into account?

- Have you organized your research using inspiration books and storyboards?
- Have you covered all areas of research and been open-minded as you proceed?
- Have you edited your research into the essential elements?

- Are you always bearing in mind the demands of the market?
- Have you made the visual impact of the final product the most important aspect of the collection?

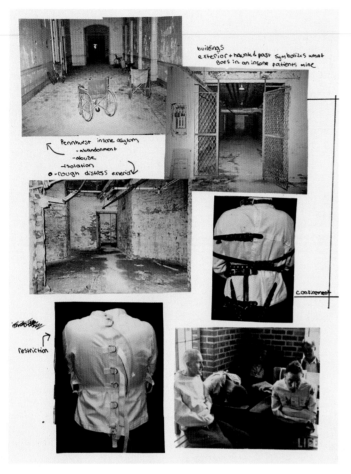

buildings
exterior + haunted past symbolizes what
goes in an insane patients mind

Pennhurst insane asylum
—abandonment
—abuse
—isolation
o — rough distress exterior

restriction

confinement

◄ 2 INSPIRATION BOARD
The history of psychiatric care
provides a clearly defined mood,
color palette, and ideas for textile,
silhouette, and detail development.
When an inspiration provides you
with enough criteria, the design
process is fluid.

2 Analysis The secondary phase allows you to analyze
how the various areas of material relate to one another.
Like the zeitgeist that often occurs among designers
in a particular season—such as the affinity for a
particular color or silhouette—you may find that you
selected elements of research subconsciously; by
looking at the material as a whole, with images on an
inspiration board for reference, patterns will emerge
and you will gain clarity for how to begin the
collection.

3 Your sketches Although your research may
provide you with a wealth of creativity and
exceptional ideas, the final product is what matters
most. Because your inspiration boards and written
text are not present alongside your garments in
the retail setting, always evaluate your work for
aesthetic appeal before anything else.

◄ 3 YOUR SKETCHES
Representation of
constraint, release,
and breaking through
barriers gives this
unified collection
a variety of design
elements. Through
the diversity of graphic
relationships and
detail placement,
the collection avoids
monotony.

Always consider the market

Remember to keep one foot in your highly creative "world" and one foot in the current market at all times. By researching current market trends and consumer behavior along with choosing relevant inspirations and themes, you will produce work that is current and desirable.

Consider also the type of inspiration your target audience will respond to and understand. This is especially important when you begin your portfolio and target particular designers or brands. What kinds of inspirations would those at Ralph Lauren or Dolce & Gabbana respond to? How would they differ from those at Comme des Garçons or Haider Ackermann, for example, and why?

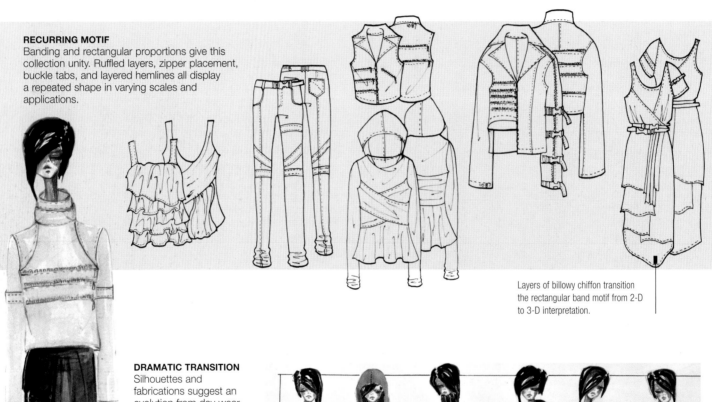

RECURRING MOTIF
Banding and rectangular proportions give this collection unity. Ruffled layers, zipper placement, buckle tabs, and layered hemlines all display a repeated shape in varying scales and applications.

Layers of billowy chiffon transition the rectangular band motif from 2-D to 3-D interpretation.

DRAMATIC TRANSITION
Silhouettes and fabrications suggest an evolution from day wear (previous page) into evening wear. A presentation becomes highly dramatic when themes develop into extreme representation.

Useful aids in the research process:

Who is your muse?

Consider for whom you are designing. How does this aspirational and fictitious person define the parameters in which all your design decisions will be made? From such designers as Ralph Lauren to Yohji Yamamoto, the lifestyle and character traits that make up this muse will help you begin developing research as you enter their imaginary worlds.

Remember the four pillars

Your research must provide the following four basic foundations on which to build a collection: mood, color, silhouette, and detail. Without these four researched elements, your collection will lack clarity, ideas will be randomly formed, and the design narrative arc will not be cohesive.

Always seek the source

The most original collections begin from the lowest "root" from which the research can be developed. Avoid giving an interpretation of an interpretation. For example, although you may have been initially inspired by the draped gowns of Madame Gres (1903–1993), you must investigate her source of inspiration, which were the draped costumes of Ancient Greece.

USING INSPIRATION BOOKS AND STORYBOARDS

As a repository for anything that sparks your interest, inspiration books should be used as a visual diary of what has triggered your creative emotions. Filing images of artwork, interiors, furniture, fashion, garment details and treatments, text, and virtually anything else will enable you to see patterns forming. These patterns may ultimately lead you to a more focused area to research and develop your next collection.

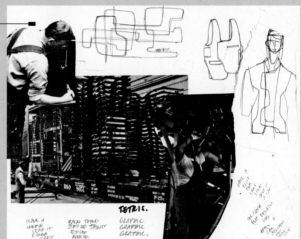

The research of automotive interiors provides the initial organic design criteria that will be used when developing this collection's motif, color, and detail.

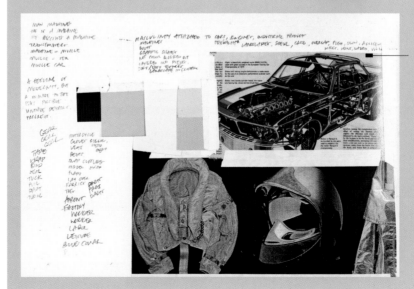

Additional research related to racing cars is incorporated to provide a richer breadth of resource. The color palette is further refined from the initial proposal above in order to convey a less graphic mood.

Color and inspiration

- **USING COLOR TO ENHANCE YOUR COLLECTION**
- **FINDING INSPIRATION FOR COLOR PALETTES**

Nothing communicates emotion more effectively than color. The context of your chosen colors can also be used to support the collection's theme and the customer profile.

olor can provide the mood, materials, silhouettes, and merchandising of your collection with strong visual and emotional resonance. Because color gives the viewer an immediate introduction to your work, the colors you use and the context in which you place them must be well chosen in order to best communicate your intended message.

Color analysis through art history

To understand how artists and designers utilize color to elicit emotion, consider shifts in art history. The various art movements were partly defined by how color relationships shifted, by the color scale, and even by how color moved the viewer's eye. As fashion designers, such considerations can have a tremendous impact on how collections are perceived. Do you want your collection to look young and athletic, or tranquil and monastic? How can an accent color create momentum during the presentation? Do certain color relationships denote particular affiliations, cultural contexts, or historical periods?

◀ WORKING WITHIN LIMITS
When a color palette is narrow, design must rely on interesting textures, diverse fabric weights, and unique silhouettes such as the cotton, suede, and contrasting mixture of drape with tailoring in this grouping.

Checklist: Using color successfully

- Have you fully considered the impact of the colors chosen for your collection?
- Have you researched art history and how colors are used in this area?

- Do you understand how color choice affects mood?
- Can an accent color be chosen to give your collection momentum?
- Have you considered the role of historical/cultural color relationships?

- Do you understand what base, supportive, and accent colors are and how they can be used?
- Have you explored the effect of the size/scale at which colors are used?

- Have you analyzed how interior designers use color?
- Do you understand the effect that color quantities and placements have on a viewer?

◀ AVOIDING STAGNATION
The concept of sportswear is built on a wardrobe that contains items to "mix and match" in order to create many looks. The designs here underscore this principle by placing color and fabrication in a manner that moves the eye and balances composition.

Consider the following when analyzing color application and its pivotal role in forming the viewer's emotional experience:

- What is the color scale, and how does this create emotion?
- What type of color palette would change the mood? Why?
- What is the artist trying to convey through color? Also with shape? Has the palette been influenced by something other than the subject matter?
- How would the mood alter if the paint were applied differently, perhaps with a more gestural or controlled hand?
- Would your emotions change if the artwork were twice as large or twice as small? Why?
- How does the color palette reflect the historical period or culture?

When you understand how artists maneuver color to underscore the subject matter and intended emotion, your aptitude for creating color stories and placements in fashion design will grow. For example, how do you feel when you see the textured color usages of Missoni knitwear or the large, clean, graphic colors used by Raf Simons for Jil Sander's spring/summer 2011 collection?

Color application

Following the initial inspiration research, a color story must be devised before the fabrics are chosen. It is critical at this stage to consider both your customer's aesthetic and the role these colors will play throughout the collection. Whether your inspiration is as rich as a Moroccan spice market (whereby the colors are copied directly from the source of inspiration) or as conceptual as a childhood memory, always consider which colors will dominate, which will support, and which will accent. For example, the color story of a fall/winter collection could include the base colors of charcoal and camel, supported by white, pale khaki, and sky blue, and then accented by pomegranate-red. The base and supportive colors are used as dominant components, while the accent color provides a rhythm to the collection in varying placements and percentages, from solid knits and blouses for layering to a thin contour line as an accent in a print.

Drawing on interior design principles

It will also prove useful to study images of interior design in order to learn about color application. Well-designed spaces may contain harmonious color palettes or highly techno and modern combinations that jar the senses. Whatever type of palette is used, designers never use color in equal measure. There will always be those that dominate and those that accent. When you understand how the quantities and placements of color affect a viewer's reactions, you will be able to use color strategically.

Assignment:
Using an interior design palette

A useful exercise is to select an image of a well-designed interior and then construct a color chart in which the scale of the colors shown on the chart represents the percentages at which they are used within the space. The chart will help you to understand the designer's color scheme and show you how to compose future palettes for your collections. Consider these key questions:

- How would you create a fashion collection based on the types of color used within the interior space?
- How and where in the collection could the accent colors be used: as piping, in prints, under layers, spun with a core-color yarn in knitwear, or as trim?
- What other creative solutions could you use to provide varying color percentages?

Choosing fabric

- **COMPOSE A FABRIC STORY**
- **MATCH TEXTILE DRAPE TO DESIGNER VISION**

Proper fabric selection is critical to give meaning to your design. It is the beginning for every collection and articulates the designer's message accurately.

▶ **ASSERTIVE CONTRASTS**
Fabrics convey a lot about your customer and the world you create. From luxurious furs to slick, techno fibers, they give clarity to your design's message.

Learning how to compose a fabric story is a true art. Like a chef with perfect technical skills who adds personality and innovation to make the familiar seem extraordinary, a fashion designer must also work on two levels: driving fashion forward, yet doing so with the technical acumen to marry form with material so every design is executed effortlessly.

Swatches of color and texture provide context for your initial inspiration and mood. The designer next advances to larger swatches: unrolling yardage from the bolt and "mock draping" on the human figure to ensure the textile's weight and drape is a happy marriage for your design. This stage is imperative before committing to a fabric and including the swatch in your croquis book.

Make the design your focus

Designs with intricate seaming and construction details often need a fabric to support without dominating the design. Either the fabric or the construction must be the design focus so they do not vie for attention and overshadow one another. Imagine using a wool bouclé for a seamed sheath dress. The sensitive line articulated through the seaming wouldn't be visible because of the fabric's texture and density. Similarly, an intricately printed floral or beaded fabric carries enough design to be used in a simple, strapless evening "column" silhouette rather than a sculptural, elaborately draped silhouette.

Let the fabric play a design role

When choosing fabrics, let the natural weight and drape dictate the silhouette and type of garment. Design lacks conviction when the appropriate weights aren't matched to the silhouettes successfully; this results in a collection that lacks both confidence and resolution, and looks amateur. If the fabric has a soft drape, avoid the temptation to tailor it. If the design is grand and sculptural, ensure that the fabric can support the form rather than relying on complicated understructures.

All fabrics have a unique personality, and accentuating these properties through cut and silhouette gives substance to your designs. Cut chiffons loose and billowy so they flaunt their weightlessness and transparency. Avoid pleating and draping bulky fabrics that are best shown in clean, tailored looks. Make the most of charmeuse and similar shiny, fluid fabrics with draping and ruching.

Checklist: Detailed fabric story

- Does your fabric story support your concept and theme?
- Does it unite the collection?
- Have you addressed your customer's needs, aesthetics, and lifestyle?

- Can your fabric story relate to the previous and following deliveries for sales floor transitioning?
- Can your fabric innovate fashion through application and/ or manufacturing techniques?

- Is it consistent with your design identity and image?
- Does the story relate to current trends while also providing an impetus for future ones?

- Does your collection contain a diverse range of fabric weights and textures?
- Does your fabric story adhere to the season while allowing for subtle shifts in temperature?

This feminine floral print was inspired by the body's internal organs and reflects the dark humor and attention to detail of the designer.

TELLING A STORY

The complex relationships of textures, weights, and colors create a dynamic fabric story. The designer's fabric development and the highly tactile nature of the fabrics underscore the collection's scientific and corporeal inspiration. Textiles can be modified with backing fabrics or constructional stitching; the true success of such adaptations will be revealed when the garments are made up and worn by models.

Vary fabric weights

Creating a fabric story that incorporates various weights ensures that silhouettes and garment constructions will not become monotonous. The thrust of a collection can be focused on tailored shapes or softer, draped silhouettes, but employing a small element of the opposite look helps communicate your primary direction. This is similar to painting: in order to show darkness, the artist must suggest a small quantity of light for contrast.

A frequent device employed by designers is to cut the same garment for a collection twice, using two different fabric weights that will give different personalities to the silhouette. For example, a trench coat might be cut in a stiff cotton canvas for day wear and in silk charmeuse for evening wear, with slightly modified proportion and detail. This not only gives the illusion that there are two designs, but it also maintains design cohesion. Plus, it is very efficient when producing patterns!

▼ CONTRAST AND COHESION

Extreme contrasts of fabric weights give this collection its eccentric, eclectic aesthetic, drawn out by bold and diverse silhouettes and varied methods of garment construction.

The croquis book:

10 essential principles

The croquis process is one of the most important aspects of fashion design. The croquis book is a visual document that displays how a collection is developed.

1 Scale

Work in an appropriate book size to show your designs clearly, neatly, and easily. The size of the figures and flats, the breadth of design per spread, and your personal comfort level within the page size all contribute to successful, rich design work. The primary goal is to show the process of your design work clearly; you don't want to turn dozens of pages in order to see a collection in its entirety.

2 Organized framework

Maintain a similar page layout throughout the book. This makes the clothing easier to focus on for the viewer. Each group should include inspiration pages, fabric swatches, 40 to 50 croquis, an accessories page, and the 6 to 8 final edits that will make up the group.

3 Clarity

Use notes, carefully drawn garments, well-rendered fabrics, swatch-accurate colors, and a suitable drawing scale to accurately depict your design intention. You will need to fit enough garments/figures per page to show the design development while ensuring that the size is large enough to see specific details.

4 Depth of context

Consider beginning the group with the more literal representations and/or the extreme aspects of the collection, and then adapt the collection as it progresses. How does the group relate to your original research in terms of silhouette, fabric treatment, fabrications, color, or garment construction? How has the group been developed into a broader context that still relates to the initial inspiration?

5 Page design

Consider whether the poses and positions of your figures direct the eye. Use windows, panels, or other graphical elements—such as negative space—to create a visual flow. The croquis book is a vessel that must engage and lead your viewer through the presentation with an aesthetic that underscores the clothes.

6 Variety and scope

A primary purpose of a croquis book is to expand initial designs and investigate options through different versions of design. Alter a garment's proportion and details, consider new ways to fabricate and coordinate the same silhouette, investigate different ways of styling, and extract details or motifs and use them in other garments to create cohesion.

7 Strategic merchandising

A well-resolved group addresses one-stop shopping. Show the different fabrics and silhouettes that will work with a design, the options for wear on a variety of occasions, and a diversity of intensities.

8 Identity

Convey a unique and well-defined personality to accentuate your design intention and bring conviction to the work. Exploit your choice of illustration medium, figure styling, layout and composition, use and style of text, and methods for adhering images and swatches onto the page.

9 Focus on the customer

Whether the groups investigate evening wear, the denim market, tailored career wear, or resort wear, consider how they relate to the designated customer's aesthetic.

10 User-friendly

Good croquis design requires immediacy and ease. Your book will be shown to many people—make sure it is sturdy enough to withstand frequent viewing, with fabrics and trims mounted securely, and ensure that your audience can review the work efficiently and effectively.

▼ THE COLLECTION ROAD MAP
Clarity, thoughtful composition, use of scale, and diverse design approaches must be successfully demonstrated. The croquis book is as much about art direction that must grab the viewer's attention as it is about the clothing designs the book contains.

14 in. (356 mm)

11 in. (279 mm)

1 Choose a book size to suit your natural drawing scale. Keep your garments and accessories in proportion on the page to draw the collection together.

2 A clean, repeating design layout keeps focus on the garments.

3 Any notes must be essential to the enterprise and easy to read.

4 Keep your design inspiration evident to a varied degree in all your work.

5 How do your figures move the eye? A full-page figure draws the eye down the page from top to bottom.

6 Show how adaptable your designs can be—borrow design details from one piece to the next and vary silhouettes.

7 Have you provided your customer with enough options? Is this one-stop shopping?

8 Allow your personality to flow through the pages in even the smallest details.

9 How is your work relevant to a particular customer?

10 Design must be clean and accessible: ensure that the book will withstand repeated viewing and is easy to look through.

LACE
ON
POCKET.

Grommit

The croquis book:
Design and structure

- **CREATE A STELLAR CROQUIS BOOK**
- **UNDERSTAND THE ROLE OF FASHION ILLUSTRATORS**

Creating a croquis book is perhaps the most important part of your role as a fashion student and design professional.

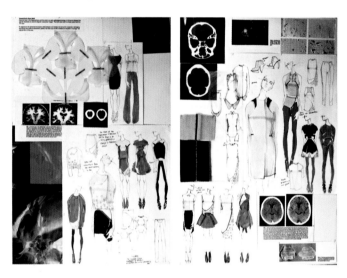

▲ LAYERING THE PROCESS
Your croquis book must contain explorations of the main elements. The high level of development shown here provides the designer with several possible approaches.

A croquis book is a means of showcasing your abilities and talents. It is a space in which you can work out your initial ideas. A croquis book reveals your unique world and documents your research process, elements of inspiration, design development, and fabric selection.

Although primarily about design development, the croquis book will also show potential employers how you make aesthetic and organizational choices. Every aspect of the book's development must be considered, from the scale of the book and the illustrations to the way in which you design the pages with visual and text-based information. When you look at the examples of croquis books in this book, ask yourself why they resonate with you:
- How do they communicate a personality?
- How does the designer approach the composition of the page?
- Why are the books interesting to look at and how do they hold your attention?

When you begin your own croquis book, decide how you wish to structure the work in order to support your overall design aesthetic. Although the book will contain many diverse group categories, which all speak to one cohesive customer, the way in which you design the book will underscore the design aesthetic of the clothing.

Checklist: Croquis book design

- Does the croquis book flaunt your design abilities and talents?
- Does the book document the research process, sources of inspiration, and fabric selection?

- Will the book show potential employers how you make aesthetic choices?
- Have you paid close attention to the composition of each page?

- Is the croquis book interesting to look at and does it hold the viewer's attention?
- Have you structured the work to support the overall design aesthetic?

- Have you considered the scale of the book?
- Have you chosen the style/medium of the illustrations carefully?
- Is the work presented clearly and neatly?

▲ GETTING SPECIFIC
Whereas figures convey the garment's silhouette and fabric behavior, flats help you realize the specifics of garment construction, design detail, and proportion.

▼ FULLY INVESTIGATED
The inclusion of 3-D process images with illustrations give clarity to your work. They flaunt your ability to work fluidly between 3-D and 2-D while testing ideas.

This croquis page allows the designer to articulate slight shifts in proportion and fit.

10 fashion illustration "greats" that everyone should know		
1	TONY VIRAMONTES	(1960–1988)
2	DAVID DOWNTON	(B. 1959)
3	STEVEN STIPELMAN	(B. 1944)
4	ANTONIO LOPEZ	(1943–1987)
5	JOE EULA	(1925–2004)
6	KENNETH PAUL BLOCK	(1924–2009)
7	RENE (RENATO) GRUAU	(1909–2004)
8	RENE BOUCHER	(1906–1963)
9	ERIC (CARL ERICKSON)	(1891–1958)
10	J. C. LEYENDECKER	(1874–1951)

• Other noteworthy fashion illustrators include François Berthoud, Mats Gustafson, Bernard Blossac, Gerd Grimm, Richard Rosenfeld, Bil Donovan, Steven Broadway, Glenn Tunstull, Ruben Toledo, John Held Jr., and many others!

Layout that supports your aesthetic

Consider retail store design. The entrance, the fixtures on which the garments hang, the furniture, the flooring, the lighting, and even the music all serve to enhance that particular designer's world and provide shoppers with a unique experience. Imagine entering a designer's boutique and the clothing has been removed. From the clean, monochromatic palette and industrial surfaces of John Pawson's Calvin Klein store in New York City to the old-world elegance of Ralph Lauren's oak-paneled drawing rooms, the interiors reflect the style of the clothing and the targeted customer. In the same way, the croquis book is designed to "contain" your work (just like a retail store).

Using the best materials

The page composition, mixture of figures with flats, and the media you choose to draw and render your fabrications all support the overall mood of your book. To familiarize yourself with the different types of medium that are available, research the work of fashion illustration from past and present. Although, in general, professional fashion illustrators are not designers, their choice of drawing media to communicate a designer's work ensures that the fabrics and overall mood are represented accurately. India ink, gouache, marker, colored pencil, graphite, collaged paper, watercolor, and even pastels can all be used alone or together to portray your work, engage your viewer, and underscore the customer you are targeting.

Instant rapport

It is not uncommon for you to be granted just a few minutes to present your work during an interview, so you must ensure that your work is understood immediately and fully appreciated.

2-D/3-D reflective process

- **DEVELOP DESIGNS BY CONSIDERING EVERY ANGLE**
- **USE DRAPES TO MAKE FINAL DESIGN DECISIONS**

An ability to work fluidly between approaches allows ideas to develop and new ones to be discovered as you move from planning to creating the garments.

During the fabric development stage, view fabrics on actual human scale. Experiment with placement and scale.

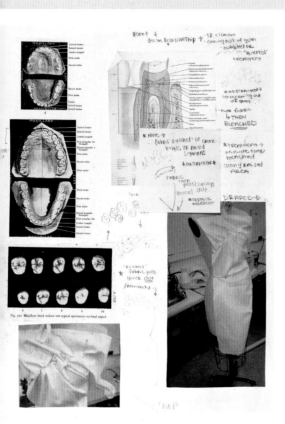

◄ **DENTAL DESIGN WORK**
The structure of teeth provides design ideas for fabric ruching and seaming. By working in 3-D, forms that are challenging to draw can be developed more easily.

For fashion design to succeed, attention to form must be a part of every decision. Fabric selection, garment proportion, and the design of the garment in its full rotation must all be considered. Although designers begin the sketching process with a front and a back, the most compelling designs are those in which every angle is thoughtfully considered. This is particularly evident in the work of the late Geoffrey Beene (1924–2004), who was initially a pre-med student. Beene's early experience of the human form made the three-dimensional design process second nature to him. This is seen in his design work and his creation of fashion that could only be truly appreciated by rotating the garment.

Using the different dimensions

Developing your work using both two- and three-dimensional approaches, as well as understanding how they can be used to support and influence each another during each consecutive step, are important skills to master. When one step is completed, the next builds on previous ideas.

Reflect on what you develop along the way and how connections can be made between processes. Being proficient in both design processes will enable you to produce designs of high resolution and depth.

Checklist: Moving from 2-D to 3-D

- Have you considered every angle carefully?
- How do the two- and three-dimensional approaches help to support and develop each other?

- Does the 2-D/3-D process give richness and depth?
- Have you continued to explore ideas while using drapes?
- Is the weight of the draping fabric the same as your final fabric?

- Is the draping fabric neutral in color?
- Have new ideas been captured that were not captured at sketching stage?

- Have you photographed the full form as well as close-ups of key areas?
- Can further garment silhouettes and design details be extrapolated from the documentation photographs?

◀ **PIECEWORK MAKES PERFECT**
A detail's scale and silhouette can display radically different designs simply by reassigning the detail's location.

Documenting your discoveries

The geometric construction of an armhole, the soft drape of a neckline, architectural seaming, the twisting fabric around the waistline, and origami folds across the bustline are all details that should be documented. As you document your draped elements, be sure to capture the process from different angles and proximities. A photograph of the full form created on the figure may provide you with a reminder, whereas close-ups of particular portions may allow you to develop ideas further.

Final questions and decisions

When you return to your croquis book, review the photographs to see how the drapes may be further developed into other garment silhouettes, and also to understand how the abstract, close-up photographs may be turned into additional design details and forms.

How might a different weight change the design? How could the initial drape proportions be exaggerated or lessened to evolve the collection? How might the placement of a draped form be shifted to provide new ideas? After further sketching, return to the form for further experimentation and to test some of your recent sketch proposals.

Getting it down on paper

The croquis process must always consist of figures, garment flats, and close-up detail shots, so that all areas of design are investigated and analyzed. After these initial ideas, silhouettes, details, and items comes the draping process, when the full rotation must be realized.

Gaining form

When you begin draping on the dress form, explore and take risks. Your initial sketches serve as a starting point, but let the forms you are creating be your primary focus. Select a fabric weight and drape that is similar to your intended fabric, such as a medium-weight muslin or a jersey that has similar body and stretch. Whatever fabric you select, always use a light-colored neutral to avoid being distracted from the process, and allow the form to be emphasized.

As you drape, rotate the form frequently and step back to gain perspective. If an element is interesting, document it and/or the full shape, then continue to evolve the work by pinning, cutting, adding, and removing. The purpose is not only to experiment with your initial ideas, but also to create new ones that the sketching process is unable to capture.

▲▶ **BEFORE/AFTER**
Although a design may begin on paper, the full 3-D realization questions, improves, and finalizes the end result.

Selection and editing:
Merchandising plan

- **CREATE A WELL-MERCHANDISED COLLECTION**
- **EDIT IDEAS DOWN TO A FINAL CAPSULE COLLECTION**

This is where the collection really starts to take shape, with the designer driven by a sense of purpose that revolves around the customer, market forces, industry protocol, and personal ambition.

Understanding how to maximize a collection's purpose relies on knowing the customer thoroughly, being aware of the direction in which fashion is going, maintaining an informed relationship with your retailers and their clientele, and creating a strategic plan for how your label's image will be developed for a consumer audience. For some designers, the collection produced for the runway serves to generate media buzz, whereas a second collection is adapted from these showpieces and produced for retail purposes. For others, the merchandising formula is strictly adhered to and dictates when deliveries are placed on the retail selling floor, as well as the ratio of garment types in the collection.

▼▶ **VARYING INTENSITY**
A collection's presentation order must be choreographed carefully to provide clear narrative and maximum crescendo. The sequence shown here begins with stiff constructed silhouettes that morph into delicate textures and prints, while offering a theatrical finale of bold motif and color.

Checklist: Merchandising a collection

- Will the collection's artistic and economic potential be realized through merchandising?
- Does the merchandising plan allow for one-stop shopping for the customer?

- Are you ensuring your potential customers stay brand-loyal?
- Do you have a strategic plan for developing your label's image for the future?

- Do the collection's components reflect varying degrees of design intensity?
- Do varied fabric weights address seasonal shifts in temperature?

- Is there an edit page showing the final looks in order of presentation?
- Have subtle changes to the edit page been accounted for before starting muslin prototypes?

Capturing your market

The core element of merchandising centers on the idea of offering your customer one-stop shopping; do not let your customer go elsewhere for a skirt, jacket, coat, sweater, or any other item that your collection should supply. A collection must provide all the different clothing components with varying degrees of design intensity and inspiration interpretation. Although the collection should be united in a mood, fabric selection, and price point, offering a more familiar silhouette of a jacket in addition to a more "forward" silhouette not only will entice two types of customer, but also will provide your core customers with an essential silhouette that serves two different occasions or moods. This is similar to offering varied fabric weights that not only address subtle shifts in temperature and diverse silhouettes, but also translate to different extremities of design on the inspiration–interpretation scale.

The edit page

Whatever the edited quantity of items per category for the final capsule collection, it is essential after the croquis stage to compose an edit page on which the final looks are shown together in the order in which they will be presented. An edit page allows the designer to make subtle changes to the group's design so that the sum of the whole is successfully resolved before advancing to muslin prototypes.

By viewing the looks together, the collection can be reevaluated in terms of color flow, texture placement, fabrication, motif manipulation, silhouette cohesion, and design intensity. For traditional sportswear collections, it is also important to analyze how items will coordinate with one another by mixing and matching them so that the customer can create a wide range of different looks.

Selection and editing:
A typical 7-look collection

The merchandising formula may vary according to such criteria as season and customer, but a typical collection will consist of core items.

▲▶ EXPERIMENTAL PRINTS
Developing fabric treatments using a variety of fabrics, scales, and colorways will provide you with options.

1 Two or three outerwear options

Outerwear offerings should include a tailored option, a shorter option, and a novelty version. An example for a fall/winter collection would be a three-quarter length camel-hair coat for professionals, a hip-length peacoat in a medium weight, wool felt with a windowpane pattern for moderate temperatures, and a cashmere-lined, nylon, hooded zip-front jacket for casual weekend wear. This category must also include items for spring/summer collections, using fabrics such as cottons, lightweight nylons, and even tropical-weight wools.

2 One or two jackets

Although not all designers offer the traditional tailored jacket, this category may be addressed primarily through the use of different fabric weights. Fabrications are limitless and include wools, cottons, leather and suede, nylons, and knits that have little give and so can be tailored. Styles could range from a pantsuit for professional occasions; a less constructed, soft-shoulder jacket in a pattern or print; a more informal, casual silhouette in leather that could also serve as outerwear; or a cropped style in a metallic fabric to transition from day to night.

3 Two or three woven shirts/blouses

The design possibilities in this category range from a simple, classic silhouette onto which other items can be layered to the more intricately designed silhouettes that stand on their own in a look. Some designers offer a range of designs and fabrications, whereas other designers provide their customer with a minimal selection because of the label's aesthetic. Particular care must be given when selecting fabrications and color relationships. A classic, crisp, white cotton shirt as a layering item; a multicolored, printed blouse in semi-sheer, silk georgette; and a jewel-tone, bias-cut, charmeuse, draped halter-top that goes from day to night is a good example of the range of fabrics and silhouettes in a capsule collection.

4 Two or three knits

Similar to the shirt/blouse category, knitwear can provide options for either layering or uniquely designed pieces that make strong statements on their own. It is essential when merchandising knitwear to offer dramatically different weights within the group so that the items on offer appeal to all your customers. A cut-and-sew jersey in a long-sleeved, T-shirt silhouette; a fine-gauge, cashmere sweater; a knit cardigan with architectural rib-knit detail; a medium-gauge, cotton sweater knit with a pattern or graphic such as variegated stripes; a suede cord that is knitted to provide an element of texture; a sculptural, chunky wool sweater used as a statement piece—these all demonstrate the diversity of knitwear.

◄ RECURRING MOTIF
Despite the varieties of fabric weights and textures that will create very different results, the well-defined shoulder silhouette and rectangular shapes give this collection cohesion.

◄ ONE-STOP SHOP
Offering your customer a variety of items will address all of her wardrobe needs.

5 Two or three pants

Including wide and slim leg, cuffed and pegged hems, pleated and flat-front waistlines, tailored trousers and drawstring-waist track pants, and even knit leggings, pant silhouettes should offer the customer various types of shapes, details, and fabrications. From a more tailored option that has a wide leg and lots of swing, and a crisp, stovepipe leg that elongates the figure and may support a large proportion on top, to a novelty fabric such as nylon or charmeuse that captures light and can address another type of category within the capsule because of its versatility, make sure that you offer versatility of silhouette and consider how fabrication reflects usage. This category also includes shorts for spring/summer collections.

▼ EXCITING DIVERSITY
With a tight color palette, the importance of diversifying texture and weight becomes essential to avoid monotony.

6 Two or three skirts

Similar to pant merchandising, skirts must adhere closely to the group's category, mood, and customer needs, and also offer varying silhouettes, fabric weights, and levels of design detail. A capsule collection must offer a versatile range of skirts that can be worn on different occasions and can be coordinated with other items.

7 One or two dresses

Depending on the customer profile and collection, the quantity and complexity of dresses may include a simple, straight sheath dress that provides color flow and/or support to a more designed piece that is layered on top, a sculpturally draped column in matte jersey that conveys a more formal presence, and a detailed summer dress in cotton voile. Consider how a dress can be its own focus through the use of design intensity and/or fabrication without the need to layer, or as a simpler silhouette that supports an item on top through the use of color or a design motif that relates to the collection.

◄ DYNAMIC JUXTAPOSITION
Design becomes dramatic when opposites collide. The weight and cocoon shape of a leather coat contrasts with a billowy chiffon dress.

Muslins and prototyping

- **MAKE THE MOST OF GARMENT PROTOTYPES**
- **STRENGTHEN THE IMPACT OF THE FINAL SELECTION**

Once the editing process is completed using illustrations, flats, fabrication, and fabric samples, garment prototypes are used to continue the development of the collection's design.

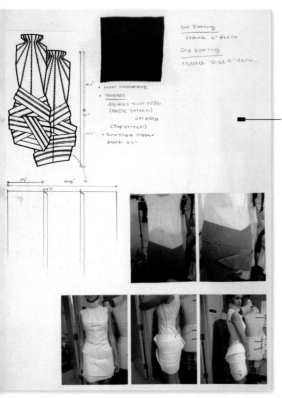

Update your notes after every fitting, and document every angle of the model for later review and pattern corrections.

The use of 3-D allows questions over design, garment fit, and initial speculations to be solved before committing to actual fabrication. Remember that your initial sketches should only serve as a foundation from which to begin the 3-D process. As your designs are realized in 3-D, your level of critical analysis must be raised; what was initially proposed on paper might not work, or you may discover better solutions and ideas. If your sketches and final collection are identical, then you are not being critical enough!

Muslins, also known as toiles, are constructed in an inexpensive fabric that is neutral in color. Make sure you use a fabric in a similar weight to that of the finished piece so that an accurate silhouette is achieved.

As you begin the draping process on the form or flat-pattern your garment, use the finalized, edited sketches as a starting point from which to develop your work. Although an idea or sketched garment

◄ RECORDING CHANGES
Documenting every step of the fitting process through notes and photos creates organization to ensure that all edits are done correctly. The use of notes, sketches, and images must all be incorporated.

Checklist: The muslin process

- Are you maintaining a strong level of critical analysis at the prototype stage?
- Does your choice of fabric weight ensure silhouette accuracy?

- Are you using the draping process to refine or improve upon the original sketches?
- Have all the looks been created in muslin before proceeding to final samples?

- Have you viewed the prototypes as a whole before making any final decisions?
- After muslin prototyping, is the collection still unified and cohesive?

- Have you allowed yourself sufficient time to develop ideas?
- Have all details such as button scale and beading layouts been reviewed?

The fit model: Typical measurements

	HEIGHT	CHEST/BUST	WAIST	HIP	SHOE
MEN	6 FT–6 FT 2 IN.	38 IN.	31 IN.	39 IN.	11–12 U.S.
	(183–188 CM)	(97 CM)	(79 CM)	(99 CM)	(45–47 E.U.)
WOMEN	5 FT 10 IN. (AND OVER)	32–33 IN.	25–26 IN.	36–37 IN.	8–9 U.S.
	(178 CM+)	(81–84 CM)	(64–66 CM)	(91–94 CM)	(38.5–39.5 E.U.)

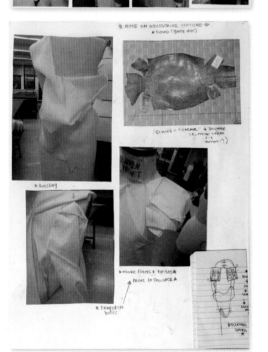

proportion may seem appealing, the execution into actual scale may be undesirable and lead you to make better choices. By no means are you required to execute your original sketch line-for-line. Use your sketches as a beginning.

It is essential to execute all of your looks in muslin first before cutting and sewing final samples. A collection is about relationships, and viewing the prototypes as a whole before committing to final decisions is critical. Doing so will ensure that the collection is unified and offers necessary momentum, while granting you enough time to develop your ideas fully.

◄ OBSERVING MOVEMENT
The fitting process allows you to perfect your patterns and evaluate the designs through the model's movement.

Always test fit in standing and seated positions.

◄ PLAYING TO DISCOVER
During your design process, use your initial drawings as a mere foundation, then explore forms in reality. The sensitive and intricate folds of these designs may have gone undiscovered had the designer adhered to pencil alone.

Muslins and prototyping:
7 important considerations

You will need to go through a set sequence of stages when developing the muslin prototypes before working on the final samples.

▲▼ ACCENTUATED FABRICATIONS

When developing your muslins, be highly cognizant of the fabrics in which they will be realized. The dramatic folds and sweeping hem of this dress will come to life in such billowy and fluid fabrications as silk charmeuse and chiffon.

1 How unified is the silhouette?
Look at the silhouettes in the collection. Is there a recurrent silhouette that creates harmony, or is there another way of creating a sense of unity? Like Dior's "A-Line Collection of Spring 1955" and his "H-Line of Fall 1954," a recurring silhouette can be used to unify the collection's theme or message.

2 Are the proposed fabric weights appropriate for the silhouettes?
Remember to unroll the bolt of fabric and "mock drape" the proportion on your body before committing to final fabrication. As the prototypes evolve from the initial sketches, reevaluate your initial fabric choices to ensure that the weaves and weights will provide the desired result.

3 How can the designer maximize the fabric's behavior?
Given the extensive choice of fabrics available, fashion designers must always be well versed in fabric types. Chiffon should be loose and billowy; shiny fabrics drape to capture light. It is often best to exaggerate a proportion during the muslin process so that

you can shorten, tighten, or lessen the effect by simply cutting away fabric rather than having to cut a whole new prototype.

4 Fittings and pattern adjustments
During the process, you may be expected to fit your looks on a live model. This will allow you not only to view your garment in true form, but also to see the design in motion. A well-trained, fit model will know where imperfections lie and how pattern adjustments must be made. This is critical because a garment will not sell if it fits badly. Conversely, some designers have loyal followers because of the excellent fit of their clothing, as is frequently seen in the denim market. After your fitting, patterns must be adjusted and finalized before fabric is cut.

5 Assessing the group as a whole
A review must be conducted when the first three and final six looks have been completed. Garments are assessed not only for proper execution, fit, and design intention, but also for the group's relationships, customer, merchandising, fabrication, motif, and narration. During the

review of the six looks, a final assessment of fabric swatches, fabric treatments, sweater knits, finishings, and fabric yardage required is conducted. Once final fabric is cut, the design process has stopped!

6 Editing: a vital consideration

Collections are always about relationships and not about individual looks. Despite the urge to keep everything you have designed and fabricated, you must be willing to edit pieces or entire looks from the collection if a subtraction makes the group stronger. It is always best to leave your audience wanting more than to feel satiated.

7 Testing every element

Before the green light is given and assessments are finalized, all fabric samples must be tested and viewed to scale. Treatments such as screen prints, knit swatches, smocking, pleating, beading layouts, button scale, and other trims must all be reviewed for final approval. Such evaluations are essential, particularly for those that are dependent upon a garment's proportion such as an engineered print.

▲ CONTEXT ANALYSIS

The purpose of the final review is to assess the group as a whole. Is the collection cohesive? Is the general mood unified? Are fabric proposals appropriate? The theatrical proportions and silhouettes of this collection result in a focused aesthetic while offering variety for merchandising.

▶ MARKED WITH STYLE

Incorporating style tape on the dress form provides a guide for intended shapes and proportions that the muslin drape will then follow. Such base markings are particularly useful when seaming detail or repeating a motif in different items.

The final samples

- **DO A FINAL ASSESSMENT OF YOUR COLLECTION**
- **PRESENT YOUR FINAL SAMPLES**

The last phase of your final collection will enable you to reflect on it in a more meaningful way and, as the garments are created, finalize decisions over styling and presentation. The principles described here are based on a final collection for a college course, but they can be applied to any collection, whether you're a student or a professional.

During the final phase of your collection, you will complete the process by making final samples. By this stage, most of the decisions about fabrications, trims, treatments, proportions, fit, and the total quantity of pieces will have been finalized. However, questions over styling and presentation will arise as the final collection is realized. Although your peers can offer a fresh perspective on its development, it may be useful to show the work to someone who is not fashion-savvy in order to get feedback or help you address areas that require better solutions.

Plotting before cutting

Before cutting your first look in fabric, you must perform a final assessment of the collection. Photograph each muslin look and place it in the order in which it will appear in the final presentation. Using a color medium such as a marker or computer, render the colors, prints, and trims intended for every garment. Is there a successful color flow? Does a fabrication or treatment need to be used more than once? Is the final collection well balanced? Does fabric placement or detail need to be reconsidered to strengthen the lineup? Performing this simple plotting technique will ensure that your final choices are successful!

Retail options

If your final collection has a print or a knit in a particular colorway, consider showing other fabric samples (known as fabric headers) as alternatives that will work within the collection. This approach is widely used when retailers place orders and opt for a different coloring, either to suit their market or so that they can offer their customers multiple options.

Outsourcing

At some design schools, students are allowed to outsource certain elements of the final collection. Beading, embroidery, leather, knitwear, pleating, dyeing, fur, and printing are all areas that may be done by an external professional if the skills needed are not part of the course or because of the technical proficiency required. If you are granted permission, you will be expected to develop a muslin

▲ **THE PERFECT FIT**
Fitting your final looks on a live model is essential before presentation due to slight changes in fabric behavior from the muslin to the actual fabric. The fitting process also gives designers one last chance to make subtle changes in design and patterns prior to production.

▶ **METHODS OF PRESENTATION**
Depending upon your program, collections may be shown statically in a gallery or on the live model during the jury process. When shown statically, it is critical that the quality of your production work is perfect!

sample and final pattern that will be sent with fabric yardage to the appropriate agency.

It is essential to allow enough time when outsourcing so that your samples will be ready for the final collection presentations. As a professional, you will be expected to submit a "spec pack," which contains the garment's pattern and explicit measurements, as well as a full garment sample so that the factory understands the garment's construction and finishing. (It's worth mentioning that although your original patterns and samples may have been made for a runway model, a production pattern and sample is also produced that is closer in size to average proportions.)

Quality standards

Prior to presentation day, you will have to submit your final collection. Your work will be evaluated by members of faculty to ensure that you have reached the required standard. It is also important to follow certain procedures for how your work should be submitted. Listed below are some basic criteria:

• The five to six looks should be on hangers, pressed/steamed, and carried in garment bags. Knits should be placed in appropriate bags to prevent stretching.
• All hems, seams, and finishes should be cleanly executed.
• There should be no safety pins, crooked hems, hanging threads or double-sided tape, or other means of finishing visible.
• No chalk marks, gathering stitches, basting stitches, pins, or lint should be visible.
• Buttons, buttonholes, zippers, snaps, grommets, and all trims must be properly applied.
• Top-stitching, embroidery, printing, and all special treatments should be neatly executed.
• Fusible interfacings must not be visible from the garment's right side. No glue or puckering should show.
• All linings should be applied correctly, and there should be no pulling or slipping out of the garment's hems.

Checklist: The final stages of the collection

• Have you fully considered the styling and general presentation of your final collection?

• Have you shown your final work to a fashion design peer and/or a non-design friend?

• Have you photographed each of the muslin looks and placed them in their running order?

• Is the color flow of the collection successful?

• Is the collection well balanced, with attention paid to fabric placements and details?

• Are you including fabric samples for prints and knits?

• Have you been granted permission for any work that needs outsourcing?

• Have you left enough time for any outsourcing work to be done?

• Are you presenting your work in the neatest, most professional way, with full attention to all stitching, seams, and details?

Accessorizing your collection

• LEARN WHAT IS
DISTINCTIVE ABOUT AN
ACCESSORIES FINAL
COLLECTION
• DISCOVER THE
DIFFERENT ROLES OF
ACCESSORIES

Accessories are the finishing touch to a graduate's final collection. They can elevate a collection to the professional category and emphasize your identity as a designer.

When your final collection is presented, your ability to convey its concept and target market will be greatly underscored by the styling. Accessories play a key role in this, while also providing your audience with a full spectrum of products that reflect the customer's lifestyle. From ergonomic and utilitarian items such as backpacks to a decorative, evening wear clutch bag to a functional but playful sun hat, accessories play a pivotal role in aesthetic communication.

Defining the role of accessories

When designing accessories, consider what role they will play within the final collection. Will they have only a supportive role or be as important a component of the collection as the clothing? Or are they simply used as a styling device? Unless you are creating an accessories collection (in which case these queries are reversed), the level of emphasis that your accessories have must be carefully considered. Accessories can play a number of roles, as follows:

A supportive role

Accessories that are based on the details, fabrications, motifs, prints, and even hardware of the clothing are often regarded as complements to the core body of work. Although the intricacies of the garments remain the primary message, accessory development typically occurs after the collection's clothing has been finalized and the design elements can then be applied to bags, shoes, hats, and even belts. Accessory designs in this category are often iconic or familiar in silhouette to prevent them from becoming a dominant visual statement, yet they employ the same colors and fabrics to blend into the final collection's thematic arc. Designers in this category include Jil Sander and Ralph Lauren.

◄ CONTRASTING SURFACES
The extreme contrast of textures provides dramatic styling. By choosing a solid black palette, emphasis is placed on the rich textures rather than complicated color relationships.

▲▶ NEAR AND FAR
When designing your accessories, it is critical to consider how changes in scale can greatly change the item. This collection contains such core accessories as shoes and bags, while successfully exploring varieties of scale, materiality, and hardware finishings.

Equal emphasis
Accessories within this range become more prominent through their intricacies and prominence of design. Rather than exhibiting the familiar shapes and details of the final collection, the designs are often as innovative as the garments themselves. The fabrications, details, and motifs of the clothing may be used in addition to new fabrications and design elements such as color, shape, texture, and detail. Although the designer's target customer remains strongly defined, the accessories convey an articulate voice that is of equal interest and design integrity as the individual fashion looks. Prada, Louis Vuitton, and other designer brands that began as accessory houses are typical of this category.

Jewelry rounds out the design offerings

Scrunched, sheer leg wear updates the overall look

Checklist: Adding accessories

• Are you using accessories to successfully underscore the main concept of the collection?

• Have you considered your target customers and how the accessories will reflect their lifestyle?

• Have you decided how prominently accessories will be used in the final collection? Will they play a supportive role or will they have a stronger emphasis (if so, see "Accessories," pages 126–127)?

• Have you taken, or do you need to take, a course in accessory design?

Minor elements

When designers wish their core collection to receive a strong focus, the choice of accessories often appears to be an afterthought. This is relevant to such avant-garde designers as Rei Kawakubo and Yohji Yamamoto, whose dramatic sculpture and innovation of the design becomes an intense visual experience. To show accessories that detract from such artistry may lessen the garments' impact, so designers often use shoes, bags, belts, and other items that are familiar and almost incognito. A simple men's brogue, a ballet flat, or other simplified shape are there purely to provide the collection with the attitude desired by the designer for that season.

Full focus

For some students, an accessories collection will be a capstone experience shown in tandem with their graduate portfolio. The final collection may encompass either one large group that speaks to a unified color and fabric story, containing a myriad of items, or multiple capsule collections that are unified by a particular theme and address several categories such as career, casual/weekend, and evening. By dividing the final collection into smaller subdivisions, fabrics and colors will vary, while always addressing the same customer profile. Whichever framework you choose, the final collection should feature between two and three garment looks alongside the accessories to communicate your customer's identity and lifestyle.

Accessory course sampling

In order to launch an accessories-based final collection or designs that simply complete the garment looks in your collection, some form of accessory design study is necessary. Courses will teach you not only how to design and produce accessories, but also the workings of the accessory design industry, both of which will give your work greater relevancy.

▲ UNIQUE APPLICATION
The unique interpretations of a similar, layered texture result in startlingly different designs for these two accessories.

▼ ADAPTABLE ACCESSORIES
The chic, youthful attitude of this look is punctuated by dramatic accessories. Customers frequently use accessories to reimagine their personal aesthetic, offer a different attitude, or complement their existing wardrobe.

Specific accessories courses

Listed below are those courses in which students are frequently able to focus on the specific and technical aspects of the accessory category at top design schools. By enrolling in such courses, you will understand how tremendously diverse the accessories market is.

- Accessories Design
- Materials Technology
- Leather Materiality
- Anatomy of Accessories
- Footwear Design and Construction
- Handbag Design and Construction
- Ergonomics for Athletic Footwear
- Accessories Computer Design
- Illustration Techniques for Accessories Design
- Small Leather Goods
- Desk Accessories
- Technical Spec and Black Line Drawing for Accessories
- Theater and Experimental Footwear
- Athletic Accessory Design
- Accessory Portfolio Development
- 3-D Model Making
- Textile Design
- History of Accessories
- Men's Accessory Design
- Children's Accessory Design

▶ **ROOTED IN SKILL**
Depending on your course, you might make your own accessories or be allowed to send them out for production. Whichever you choose, knowledge of the process will give you greater creative insights for future design work.

▶ **DRAMATIC EXPECTATIONS**
Accessories may veer far from the expected categories of shoes and bags. Some designers may include one-of-a-kind art pieces and/or designs that contribute solely to the collection's runway presentation.

Styling

- **STYLE A COLLECTION SUCCESSFULLY**
- **UNDERSTAND HOW GOOD STYLING ENHANCES A COLLECTION**

Successful styling will elevate your work to a more contextual level, but it should not compete for attention with the collection's garments in any way.

▲ **STYLING THROUGH PROPS**
Suggestive props allude to this collection's unmistakable theme. By keeping the background neutral, the dramatic colors and silhouettes garner maximum focus.

After an intensive period of creating a final collection, it is essential that the designs provide the emotional and visual impact you intended. As a primary tool for conveying this vision, styling is one of the final elements to consider, and its importance cannot be stressed enough. Consider your reaction when viewing runway shows or editorial layouts that utilize accessories, hairstyles, makeup, and even props to convey an artistic message. How does the art direction transport you from an ordinary item such as a peacoat into a world that inspires and excites you? What is it about the styling that makes you remember the work for years to come?

Different styling approaches

The ways in which you style your collection can be determined by many factors. For some designers, a reinvestigation of their historical inspiration can provide useful material to help them select appropriate accessories or hairstyles. Other designers choose to focus exclusively on the mood they wished to suggest and let the garments speak for themselves through choices of lighting, slicked-back or tousled hair, makeup, and other decisions that reflect the customer's world. Another approach might be to employ styling elements that contrast with the designs in order to heighten the

relationships and thereby display the intended message more clearly. For example, if a designer wants his or her audience to focus on extravagant drapery techniques, a small element of construction in the collection will accentuate the focal area.

By considering every possible element for how you want your collection read, you can guide your viewer's perceptions without risking misinterpretation or a banal reaction. Similar to the way in which a collection is developed, listing inspirational adjectives will help you develop your styling decisions.

Checklist: Styling techniques

- Does the styling underscore the visual and emotional impact you set out to achieve?
- Have you used good art direction to enhance your artistic message?

- Does the styling give the collection a stronger focus?
- Does the styling successfully guide the viewer or is it confusing?

- Are the styling elements strong enough to convey the message alone?
- Do the styling choices compete for attention with the garments?

- Does your choice of styling make you stand out from the crowd?
- Have all possible styling techniques been exploited?

The 4 hallmarks of successful styling

Bear in mind the following key points when styling your collection:

1 Underscore the mood and theme
Like a food stylist who selects particular props to tell a story about a certain dish, the styling should accentuate the collection's narrative and mood. What are you trying to say with your collection? Imagine that only the hair, makeup, location, lighting, and accessories were on display. How do these elements suggest what the clothes would look and feel like?

2 Let the styling be secondary
Successful styling acts as the bass guitar to the primary melody. Your styling choices are noted, but they do not compete for attention with the clothing designs or leave the audience confused about what they should be examining. For example, you do not want your viewers to be enthusing about the hairstyles or makeup techniques and view the fashion as an afterthought! At the same time, unique styling choices and combinations can separate you from the countless other fashion designers trying to make their mark.

3 Deepen meaning
One of the best places to learn about styling is at the theater, particularly when the set and costume design isn't literal and the designers have been given full license to be abstract. How do lighting, color, texture, and form affect your emotions? How do these emotions then mirror the performance's plotline and individual characters? The purpose of styling is to elevate your design and provide a stronger, more focused message.

4 Guide to your approach
Consider how designers such as Michael Kors and Rei Kawakubo style their collection. Using hair, makeup, and accessories, as well as the choreography of the model's walk, also informs how the viewer should approach the work. The fun and flirtatious walk at Kors gives the clothes a sense of American approachability, whereas the monastic "street-walk" at Comme des Garçons instills a serious mood that encourages the viewer to engage cerebrally with the highly innovative creations.

The look book

- **CREATE A MEMORABLE LOOK BOOK**
- **CHOOSE PHOTOGRAPHERS AND MODELS**

The look book, in addition to proving to be indispensable in interviews, is an essential marketing tool and will be an important part of your presentation.

▲▼ **RUSTIC URBAN**
The organic and earthy textures of this collection gain maximum effect when situated in an urban, industrial setting. Placing a collection's context within a contrasting external context can strengthen the desired mood.

Checklist:
Creating a look book

- Have you collected inspirational images to help your art direction?
- Have paper choices, layout, and typography been adequately considered?
- Have you looked at location choice, lighting techniques, and model poses for inspiration?
- Does the design of the book accentuate the collection's vision?
- Does your chosen photographer's artistic vision agree with yours?
- Does your photographer share the same professional approach?
- Have you briefed the photographer properly?
- Do you need to use a model to convey your message?
- Does your selected model reflect the personality of your collection?

Every season, designers produce printed material or look books to showcase their collections. These look books are distributed to the press, retailers, and publications so that the recipients can then request items for photo shoots, place purchasing orders, and write reviews. Look books usually contain images shot directly from the runway to offer the clearest depiction of the styled looks. Accessories may be photographed separately and placed at the back of the book. Some designers produce a second book that places the work in a context and gives it a particular mood through the use of settings, props, and artistic photography, which will then be given to customers as advertising material.

Designing your look book
When your collection is finished, you will have to document the work. During the months leading up to your final collection

presentation, collect any imagery, printed material, and photography that inspire you. Types of paper and finishings, layout compositions, typography, types of styling, settings/locations, lighting techniques, model's poses, and even movie stills or fine art can all provide inspiration for the art direction and production of your look book. Consider also how the design of the book can be used to accentuate the collection's vision and increase its appeal.

Finding a photographer

If you have fellow students who are studying photography, then this can be a highly successful collaboration; you will receive printed material, while your peer will gain images for his or her own graduate portfolio. However, before selecting photographers, view samples of their work to ensure their vision and aesthetic will complement your own. It is also critical that you work with someone who is equally professional and committed to the project.

The model and collection's personality

You will also need to decide if a model is required and how you will select the appropriate one. Never underestimate how critical your model is for conveying the aesthetic of your work. He or she is often the first indicator of a collection's personality. The cleanliness seen at Jil Sander, the W.A.S.P. look of Ralph Lauren, and the sexiness of Gucci, for example, are all the result of art direction that supports the designers' visions. Consider who your target customer is and whether she wishes to see either the woman she aspires to be or a representation of a concept that she wishes to engage with intellectually. For some designers, such as Comme des Garçons, the use of real people on the runway suggests a reaction against the glamorous worlds seen at such houses as Valentino and Armani.

Checklist: Choosing a photographer

- Which photographers and artists inspire the photographer and his or her work?

- Have a lengthy conversation with the photographer about art, design, your work, and methods of working.

- Is there a natural connection between you? Does the photographer understand your aesthetic approach and goals for the project?

- How much creative freedom will your photographer be granted? Will you collaborate on the project or are you simply looking for someone to serve as a technician?

- How can researched images of photography or other material convey your intended aesthetic and mood? Can text or visual diagrams, for example, help your photographer achieve the desired results?

- Is this an equal exchange or is another form of compensation required?

The look book
10 essential principles

Your look book needs to have a high aesthetic impact. Consider these guidelines before you start the design process.

◄ FASHION COMMUNICATION
Although your book's art direction can be highly personalized, clear depiction of the garments is priority. You may include multiple shots of the same garment, standing and seated poses, as well as close-ups for unique details.

▼ KIDDING AROUND
The look book does more than just show your collection. It identifies your brand's attitude within the entire market. Playful use of props, images, and choice of model are all key communicators in this book.

1 Decide on a scale
How do you respond when opening a book of images that is the size of a deck of cards or as large as a newspaper? Does one appear more intimate or elicit a particular mood? Scale creates an experience for your viewers, so consider how you wish them to feel when viewing your book. Will it be intentionally dramatic by being very large or small, or less of a statement by being more manageable in size?

2 Get the styling right
From the real-life, approachable aesthetics of Ralph Lauren and Miu Miu to the theatrical worlds of Comme des Garçons and John Galliano, how you style your collection should generate interest in your target customer, while emphasizing how you wish to be perceived as a young designer.

3 Present the look book creatively
How you present the work will engage the viewer in different ways. Although most designers use a simple book format, others might put loose cards in a well-designed box. For example, a collection with a tropical theme could keep printed postcards in a woven box with a vial of sand inside. The book might stand alone or be kept in a bag made from fabric used in the collection.

► AMPLIFY YOUR MESSAGE
A clean, bold cover introduces the viewer to the graphic aesthetic that is the hallmark for this collection. The white background accentuates the clothing's graphic silhouettes.

4 Select the best setting

When you view advertisements, how does the setting create a mood and connect with the targeted viewer? Is there a setting or is it nonreferential? Why would the advertisements of Alexander McQueen feature fantasy settings, whereas DKNY uses identifiable scenes of New York City? Remember, however, that a white backdrop often works best.

5 Use props with care

Like settings, props can add weight to your message and aesthetic. From a butterfly net for a childrenswear group inspired by a summer garden to a baroque chair used to suggest a customer's taste, props offer endless possibilities. Make sure that they don't overpower the image.

6 Compose the pages thoughtfully

An empty space without an image is just as critical as filled space. How do you feel when images are playfully scattered on the page or when they are uniform and given large quantities of white space around them? Does it make you perceive the collection differently? How you arrange images and text on the page will provide further aesthetic direction to show who you are as a designer.

7 Choose the best materials

Although it may seem unimportant, the type of paper or other material on which the look book is printed can influence the viewer's perception of the collection. High-gloss, stark-white paper may be appropriate for some collections, whereas others may seem incongruous on such a choice. You should also decide whether you want your look book to emphasize clarity or mood. For example, printing on a paper that affects the color accuracy of the fabric may enhance the collection's mood but compromise the representation of the garments' colors.

8 Entice your target audience

What will your targeted viewers respond to most and why—a highly stylized photo shoot complete with setting and props in which they can imagine themselves; a white, gallery-type room that emphasizes the fabrics, colors, and details with the most clarity; or a fantasy narrative that places mood and imagery above clear garment depiction to encourage closer examination? Like choosing inspiration for a collection, be highly sensitive to what your customers will be most excited by in order to draw them in.

9 Amplify the mood

Like the music during a movie that leads the viewer's emotions, mood is directed through lighting, photography genre, model's pose, and even the positioning of the camera. How your viewer reacts emotionally to your collection is largely dependent upon your carefully directed images.

10 Always be innovative

Like everything in fashion, do what's new within the context of your aesthetic and target market. Although you may use a traditional format, how can you provide an updated version that excites your audience? Conversely, if the clothing has such a powerful direction, clean and simple may be the best route for the art direction to avoid diluting the message and competing with the garments themselves.

_ DESIREE N EMAN.

Layout and design

The look book's design must be considered carefully in order to successfully communicate your work. There is perhaps no better example of this than the visual experience designers create within their own boutiques. Styling must be carefully chosen so that it showcases the clothing in the best possible context.

◀ SEVERE SILHOUETTES
The spliced images and segmented compositions underscore the theme of reconstructed garments and conveys a modern customer. When designing the book, how could setting, lighting, image placement, and the model's poses allude to your collection's theme without appearing literal?

▼▶ MAKING IT INTERACTIVE
A book does not always need to follow a conventional book format, yet it must always be easy for the viewer to review. This accordion-style presentation allows the viewer to interact spontaneously with its dramatic, sweeping layout. Consider how the reverse side could show images of mood, process, or even your current résumé.

▶ EFFECTIVE SPACE

Aside from using a striking location to support the theme, this layout uses varied negative space for dramatic effect. Negative space is just as important as the positive, printed area. By varying these spaces, your viewer becomes engaged and excited due to the unpredictable (yet cohesive) layout.

Final presentation and evaluation

- **WHAT TO INCLUDE IN A FINAL YEAR COLLECTION**
- **STRUCTURING AN EFFECTIVE PRESENTATION**

The presentation of your final year collection marks the end of your undergraduate education and your debut into the professional world.

At the end of your final year, you may have to present your final collection, potentially to a body of jurors. Those in attendance may include professional designers, retailers, journalists, school alumnae, and job recruiters. The presentation may also serve as your first interview, as many jurors attend graduate shows in the hope of finding new talent for their own labels. Every college has its own procedures, but a typical presentation length is around 10 minutes.

▼ BACK TO BASICS
Before you consider what your verbal presentation will be, revisit your initial notes and research. By refreshing your memory, you will be able to create a meaningful and concise summary of the key points you wish to make to your audience.

< MOOD >
CREATE NEUTRAL COLORED CLEAN CUT AND ELEGANT GARMENTS ACCENTUATING KNOTS, TWISTS AND DRAPERY ON GARMENTS REFLECTING THE SHAPES OF NATURE AND COMPLEXITIES OF HUMAN EMOTIONS. THE GARMENTS ARE LIGHT, AIRY AND THEY FLOW OVER OUR WOMEN'S BODY WITH EASE YET WITH METICULOUS DETAILS.

< MUSE >
SHE IS FREE, UNTAMED, STRONG AND YET EXTREMELY FEMININE. SHE IS AN INTERIOR DESIGNER, HER CLIENTS INCLUDE FAMOUS CELEBRITIES SUCH AS SARAH JESSICA PARKER AND ROBBIE WILLIAMS. HER DESIGN PHILOSOPHY IS TO CREATE EUROPEAN STYLE FURNISHINGS WITH COMFORTABLE AND WARM SURROUNDINGS REPRESENTING AMERICAN LIFE STYLE. DUE TO HER CAREER, SHE OFTEN TRAVELS AROUND THE WORLD; HER BUSINESSES ARE BASED IN EUROPE AND AMERICA, SO SHE SPENDS A LOT OF TIME ABROAD. FOR HER CAREER IS AN IMPORTANT PART OF HER LIFE BUT SHE IS NOT A PRISONER OF IT. SHE IS FINANCIALLY SECURE, SO SHE IS ENTITLED TO EVERYTHING THAT MONEY CAN BUY. HER MOTTO IS TO LIVE FOR TODAY, NOT FOR TOMORROW. SHE ENJOYS CLOTHES THAT ARE EDGE, ELEGANT YET SOPHISTICATED. SHE ADORES SILKY, AIRY DRESSES WHICH NATURALLY FLOW AROUND HER BODY LIKE OCEAN WAVES, ACCENTUATING HER SHAPELY FIGURE. SHE IS INVITED TO MANY PARTIES FROM THE RICH AND FAMOUS AND THAT IS WHEN SHE LOOKS AT HER BEST WITH HER ELEGANT TASTES IN FASHION. ALSO SHE TAKES FASHION SERIOUSLY BECAUSE SHE BELIEVES THAT MODERN WOMAN HAS RESPONSIBILITY TO LOOK AT HER BEST AT ALL TIMES.

< NATURE'S SATISFACTIONS AND HUMAN'S EMOTIONS >
INSPIRATION COMES FROM FORMATIONS AND SHAPES OF NATURAL PHENOMENON, SUCH AS WAVES OF OCEAN, AND STRATIFIED ROCKS. THESE NATURAL SHAPES AND LINES CAN ALSO BE SHOWN TO INDICATE VERY CHARACTERISTICS OF HUMAN EMOTIONS. AS THE TIDES COME AND GO OUT OF THE OCEAN FLOOR, THE SAND IS LEFT WITH THE WAVY SCARS. HUMAN COULD ALSO BE LEFT WITH EMOTIONAL SCARS, WHEN ONE IS FACED WITH VARIOUS LIFE EXPERIENCES.
HOWEVER, AS THE WAVE WASHES AWAY THE SAND, THE SCARS ARE FLATTENED, THEY DISAPPEAR.
OUR EMOTIONS ARE SIMILAR WITH THIS MOVEMENT BECAUSE OF SENSATIONS WE FEEL ARE OFTEN TEMPORARY.
JUST LIKE THE WAVES, OUR EMOTIONS COME AND GO IN OUR MEMORY LANE AND LEAVE DIFFERENT MARK EACH TIME AND THEY ARE ERASED MOST SIMULTANEOUSLY. STRATIFIED UNRESOLVED FEELINGS THAT WE PRESS DEEP IN OUR HEARTS, WHICH CAN LEAD TO VIOLENT CORRUPTION IN OURSELVES. THE VISIONS OF NATURE AND HUMAN EMOTIONS SHOW INTERESTING SIMILARITIES.

▶ **QUALITY CONTROL**
Assess your technical skills before you begin your thesis so that your collection's quality will be the highest possible. This collection balances complicated construction with simpler silhouettes to maintain a manageable workload for the designer.

Checklist: What you will be marked on

- Is the fabric choice appropriate to customer and silhouette?

- Is this "one-stop shopping"? How well merchandised is the collection?

- Are the silhouettes and fabrics season appropriate?

- How successfully are texture, color, and pattern handled?

- Are there enough weights of fabric?

- How well edited is the group? Is there redundancy (silhouette, fabric, and so on) or room for expansion? How/Why?

- How do fabrics and silhouette relate to inspiration? Are the choices effective?

- How well defined is the customer?

- What would you have done to make the collection stronger (color, silhouette, fabric choice, styling, the presentation order, editing, etc.)?

- Are the pieces accurately priced for the target market? Are they appropriate for the collection?

Deciding what to include

Remember, your jurors are fashion experts. Describing the pocket type chosen or the size of a button isn't interesting to people who look at countless collections each season. But information about your inspiration, methods of fabric development, or how a garment can transition into various silhouettes are worth mentioning because they are unique to you, enabling jurors to connect with the collection on an emotional and personal level.

By considering the following criteria, you will be including essential information, while also giving yourself scope to add personal material that will set you apart from the other graduates:

1 Introduce the group
Include the inspiration/theme(s), colors used (and why), fabrics used (and why), and motif extracted from the inspiration and how this was manipulated in the group.

2 Describe your customer
Who is he or she? Is there a reason you selected this particular customer? (Provide a character sketch that describes his or her life, age, demographics, stores he or she shops in, and so on.) Why do you consider this modern, and how/why does it reflect the future of fashion design? Be prepared to back up your answers with research, whether trend focused or sociologically focused.

3 The collection
Who are your competitors? Work this out using information on similar customer taste/identity, price points, retailers, and designers sold in your retail area. State your price range, i.e., the wholesale and retail prices of a tailored jacket, dresses, pants, basic tops, and sweater knits, which are the benchmarks for a collection's price point. (Remember, your prices should mirror those of your competitors.) Which stores (and floors) do you envisage your work being sold in/on?

4 Show the collection: The sales pitch
Draw attention to details and any interesting techniques (Construction? Printing? Dyeing? Knits?). Highlight selling points, for example, merchandising issues, versatility, time of day, customer appeal. At this stage you must excite your audience and explain why your collection is unique.

5 And lastly...
Remember, you've worked hard over many years for these 10 minutes, so make the most of them as both an educational experience and a chance to debut into the professional world!

Presentation day

On the day of your presentation, you might present in your school's auditorium, classroom space, or other location the college has set aside. Your jurors may be given ballots along with a list of criteria for how the work should be assessed. After each session, ballots should be collected and tallied. Once all students have presented their collection, colleges usually select the top-scoring students to be nominated for a "Designer of the Year" award, which could lead to further opportunities to present their work to highly esteemed figures in the fashion industry.

▼ COVERING ALL AREAS
Utilizing the accessories you have designed for your collection is essential when presenting your thesis. The clothing, accessories, and even how you style the model's hair must all connect into one defined and focused point of view.

Preparing a 10-minute presentation

Using your collection work to date, assume you have to prepare for a forthcoming presentation. To make maximum impact, consider adopting the following strategies:

1 Plan for a 7-minute commercial
Split the 10 minutes into 7 minutes to present the work and 3 minutes to allow your jurors to ask questions, offer support, and give constructive criticism. You will be challenged and expected to explain your work and decisions, as well as the overall process of realizing the collection. Also prepare questions to ask the panel in case they are less than forthcoming such as "How could my collection be strengthened?" and "Where should I focus on, professionally?"

2 Prepare the defense
The jurors may ask you about the decisions you made, whether these pertain to fabrics chosen, details developed, cohesion of the looks, or the general narrative proposed. You must have a reason and explanation for everything, so come fully prepared to explain your decisions.

3 Practice makes perfect
Practice your presentation in front of your peers (both fellow fashion undergraduates and those doing different courses), asking them to challenge you with difficult questions. By rehearsing several times, you will remember everything you want to say, while also flawlessly executing the choreography required when showing garments.

Final Collection Review Presentations
Tuesday, 10:00–12:00

Presenter	Poor Excellent	Designer of the year Candidate? Y / N
1. John Sedgwick	1 2 3 4 5 6 7 8 9 10	Y / N
2. Alex Jones	1 2 3 4 5 6 7 8 9 10	
3. Jill Steward	1 2 3 4 5 6 7 8 9 10	
4. Jason Lovinsky	1 2 3 4 5 6 7 8 9 10	
5. Noel Callen	1 2 3 4 5 6 7 8 9 1	
6. Marilyn Gough	1 2 3 4 5 6 7 8 9	
7. Richard Rosen	1 2 3 4 5 6 7 8	
8. Steven Porter	1 2 3 4 5 6 7 8	
9. Grace Goodman	1 2 3 4 5 6 7	
10. Andrew Talbot	1 2 3 4 5 6 7	
11. Nolan Beckford	1 2 3 4 5 6 7	
12. Louise Gillman	1 2 3 4 5 6	
13. William Santisi	1 2 3 4 5	
14. Jackie Newman	1 2 3 4 5	
15. Barbara Spinelli	1 2 3 4	

Designer of the Year Ballot

Student's Name: _____

	Poor Excellent
Final Collection	1 2 3 4 5 6 7 8 9 10
Croquis Book	1 2 3 4 5 6 7 8 9 10
Portfolio	1 2 3 4 5 6 7 8 9 10
Innovation	1 2 3 4 5 6 7 8 9 10
Identity	1 2 3 4 5 6 7 8 9 10
Conceptual Thinking	1 2 3 4 5 6 7 8 9 10
Consistency	1 2 3 4 5 6 7 8 9 10

Juror Notes:

◄ **JURY DELIBERATIONS**
Procedures differ between colleges, but your jury might use ballots like these during your review. Criteria for rating your work will be based on customer suitability, creativity, innovation, execution, and presentation. Competition will be fierce, and you must excel in all areas during your "debut" into the professional world.

▼ **THE THESIS LIFE CYCLE**
The presentation of your thesis collection does not end after the jury and/or fashion show. It will become a key component to your graduate portfolio and may be shown for years to come. As such, it should deeply reflect who you are as a future designer.

Maximizing your portfolio

As the primary sales tool for your talents, your graduate portfolio provides visual evidence of your skills. Its evolution must be continuous in order to best reflect your views on where fashion is headed.

The portfolio should provide your viewer with a view of your creative self. Your aesthetics, work ethic, attention to detail, ability to solve problems, and even the kind of employee you will be are all indicated in the portfolio's presentation. Like the clothing we choose to wear, your portfolio shows the world who you are. In addition to its contents and how they are presented, a myriad of other factors must be considered so that your viewer is excited by your work and the message remains focused.

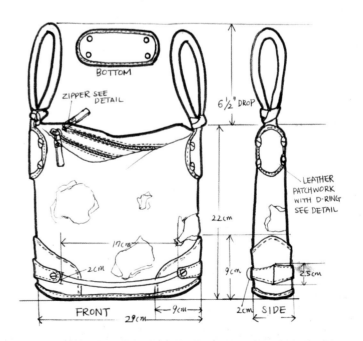

Optimum portfolio presentation

• **CREATE AN EFFECTIVE PORTFOLIO**
• **PRACTICAL CONSIDERATIONS FOR A PORTFOLIO**

To get the best outcome from a well-designed portfolio, you will need to take certain design and content criteria into account.

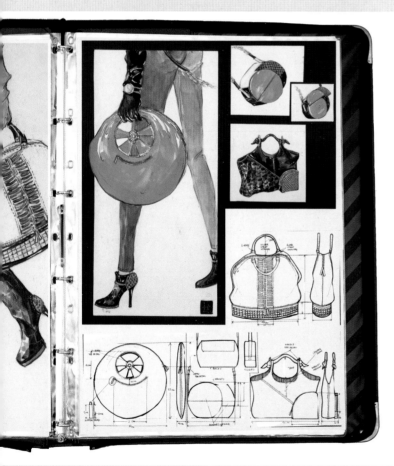

It is important that you only show work executed during your final year, because your skills will have improved and the viewer wishes to see your most recent design work. If your previous work is truly exceptional and equal in quality to your current work, then consider including it.

Knowing how much or how little to include is an important skill to develop. Too little work and you appear to lack creativity; too much and you overwhelm your viewer while also demonstrating poor editing skills. Remember to avoid showing irrelevant material such as fine art, life drawing, non-fashion photography, and illustration work that is not connected to fashion design and the position you are interviewing for. Such work may deter from your portfolio's message, look amateurish, and potentially make you appear unfocused in your career goals.

In terms of content, the ultimate portfolio sin is to show group after group that use the same predictable framework. Varying figure poses, scales, backgrounds, quantities of pages and figures per group, art direction, and even mediums will not only entertain the viewer with sudden surprises, but also flaunt your diversity and creativity for presenting work. Well-chosen art direction will also underscore each group's theme and overall mood. Avoid being predictable!

◄ FLAUNT IT
These flats, with specific measurements, demonstrate a good understanding of accessory design. Flaunting knowledge and skills throughout your book is mandatory for landing a job.

Checklist: Strong portfolio development

• Are you showing your most recent design work?

• Is any previous work included that is of the same quality as your current work?

• Have you included the right amount of work, i.e., neither too much nor too little?

• Is all the material included relevant?

• Is the art direction appropriate to the theme and mood?

• Does the presentation of the different groups show enough variation?

• Are the physical dimensions of the portfolio suitable?

• Is the portfolio easy to look at and review?

• Does the portfolio start with work that makes the viewer eager to see more?

Practical considerations

Consider the following when curating your book:

Choose the right size

Before starting any design or illustration work, choose a portfolio size that's right for you. Like the look book, the size, format, cover, and even type of paper you choose will all affect the viewer's engagement with and feelings toward your work. In general, the portfolio book should be no larger than 14 x 17 in. (36 x 43 cm) and no smaller than 9 x 12 in. (23 x 30 cm); 11 x 14 in. (28 x 36 cm) is a popular size.

Is the portfolio user-friendly?

Make sure that the portfolio is easy to review. Avoid complicated fold-outs and check that the fabrics and trims are mounted securely. Ensure that all the information is non-verbal, and that the work is easy to understand and goes in one direction. Remember, neatness counts along with a professional and well-art-directed presentation. Even the way you cut and mount your swatches must be given artistic consideration.

Use exciting bookends

Begin and end with your best work, with a peak in the middle. Your first group often shows your quality as a candidate and if you are to be taken seriously. Will your viewers continue to peruse with undivided attention, or can they tell from the first group that you are not qualified? The first group should also provide a gradual entry into your aesthetic domain with the following groups offering momentum and spontaneity. Like a movie's final scene, your closing group is often what viewers remember most.

▼ **INCLUDE YOUR THOUGHT PROCESSES**
Successful portfolios and croquis books display much of the creative process. This page is highly effective due to its use of notes alongside images that explain textile developments.

Show variations of an idea to offer choice

The stellar portfolio:
9 ways to stand out

Understanding what makes a portfolio stand out from the rest is essential if you are to compete in today's talent pool.

◀ INSPIRED BY ART
This presentation style was inspired by the work of illustrator Edward Gorey. By researching other forms of art or design and interpreting them in your portfolio development, a unique result is likely.

1 Always evolving

Many designers are considering their next collection as they finalize the current one. This focus on the future enables them to foresee the direction in which fashion will swing. Similarly, it highlights the importance of striving to create stronger work that is an evolution of the designer "self." Although your portfolio may appear finished, constantly update your work to hone your vision, while simultaneously producing work that relates to the current market.

2 A non-verbal you

Although the main purpose of the portfolio is to showcase your fashion design abilities, it also reveals your views about fashion and society, your problem-solving skills, your level of professionalism, and, to a degree, your personality. When showing evidence of your skills, include illustration work, technical drawings (or flats), 2-D and 3-D work, digital work such as illustration and textile design, fabric treatment and knit samples, etc.

3 Editing for change

A portfolio typically contains six to eight groups. However, by developing a few external groups that can be used as replacements, the book's context can shift greatly. This is useful when your book needs to target a specific house. By replacing groups, rearranging the order and pace, and reconsidering the book's overall arc, you can successfully target prospective employers. Consider which houses might prefer more innovative collections and which might appreciate more saleable and commercial designs.

4 Keeping the currency

Employers never want to see what is currently being shown; they are only interested in seeing new ideas, high levels of creativity, and a designer with a strong point of view. With this in mind, update your portfolio at least every six months, even if you are not looking for a position.

5 Art direction

Use good art direction to ensure that your portfolio is about the viewer's experience as a whole, and not just about fashion design. It must vary throughout the book to avoid becoming monotonous, yet arise from the same design aesthetic. Figure compositions, choices of paper, scale, illustration styles and media, and page arrangement are just some of the areas to consider in order to diversify your groups' formats.

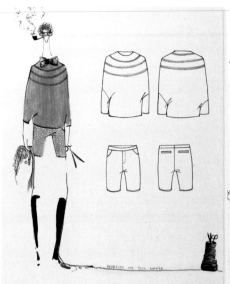

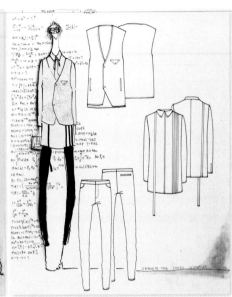

6 Unify and diversify

Although a portfolio may contain many different groupings and seasonal deliveries, they must all be united through a specifically targeted muse and aesthetic; demonstrate varied inspirations, color and fabric palettes, design intensities, and market categories; and provide the customer with "one-stop shopping." Avoid a repetition of design approach to show that you are full of ideas and able to design to any type of criteria. This is a highly sought-after skill by employers!

7 Entertainment

Consider how you will excite, engage, and even entertain your audience when they review your book. Each group must offer a unique experience that highlights the group's theme and mood. Some groups may be illustrated conventionally, whereas others may be vaguely suggestive of the garments and gestural in style. Some portfolios may include interactive features such as paper doll cutouts or transparent paper that slowly dress the model underneath.

8 Well paced

A successful fashion show producer creates momentum as a collection is presented. Similarly, your portfolio should offer different design intensities and build up to a crescendo. Allow the first group to be a gradual entry into the book's aesthetic, and let the final group maximize your creativity. Between these bookends, you can display the range of your capabilities as a designer. Groups ranging from sportswear, knitwear, resort wear, activewear, accessories, and even textile design all provide various types of design experiences.

9 Now break the rules!

Innovation often means breaking the rules, and this is especially true in the fashion design world. This includes moments in fashion history when someone suggested new, more exciting ideas for the use of fabrics, the design of retail stores, how people experience fashion, and even traditional manufacturing. There are no rules in fashion design except that you must always know who your audience is and what they will appreciate. The rest is negotiable, which means that you can produce an innovative product and portfolio presentation.

▲ CHARACTER SKETCHES
A unique illustration and presentation style conveys a particular attitude in this menswear collection. Avoid repetitious layout design among your groups to keep the viewer entertained. Layout design and different paper and mediums can all catch attention.

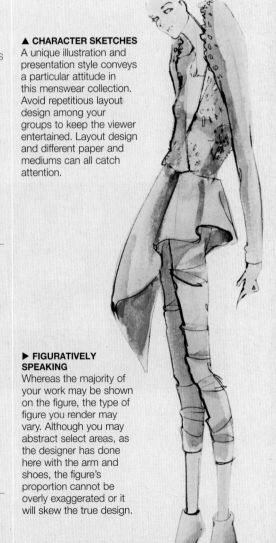

▶ FIGURATIVELY SPEAKING
Whereas the majority of your work may be shown on the figure, the type of figure you render may vary. Although you may abstract select areas, as the designer has done here with the arm and shoes, the figure's proportion cannot be overly exaggerated or it will skew the true design.

Web presence

Although conventional marketing tools are essential for self-promotion, the technologies that created social media have revolutionized the job market, and you'll need a firm grip on the online opportunities available to you.

Traditionally, creating a brand draws on many specialties, including marketing, advertising, business networking, and ensuring clear product differentiation and strong aesthetic associations with your brand name. Although these tools are all still fundamental, the virtual world is becoming just as important for the development of your brand.

Whatever avenues you choose, make sure that your websites, ads, and pages drive viewer interaction and engagement. Regularly add new content, particularly photos and videos. Include a mailing list sign-up section in which you offer subscriber-only content or previews of new collections. Include message boards on your site, enabling viewers to comment on your work and connect with other viewers. Remember, engaging viewer interaction is critical for both acquiring and maintaining customers.

Familiar headings create a user-friendly tone and give browsers key information quickly.

A well-conceptualized logo grounds your creative mission, which will be sustained in years to come.

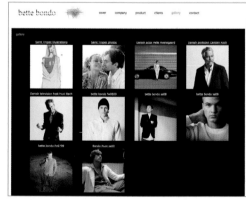

◀▲ CYBER YOUR AESTHETIC
For some customers, their first impression of your brand will be through your webpage and to display this in a concise, direct manner may increase loyalty and sales.

Selected images on your homepage provide an immediate insight into your aesthetic and give an overview of your diversity.

Online advertising

Researching the best advertising methods will help sustain your brand's commercial success.

Google AdWords

This is both a business and a universe unto itself. Google AdWords enables you to choose specific search queries, such as "audreycouture," "edgy fashion," or any other permutation of descriptive words, which could be associated with your brand. You purchase bids on specific keywords and have the option to pay either every time your ad pops up in a Google search or every time someone clicks on your ad. Visit adwords.google.com for more information. If you want to drive immediate traffic to your site, you should strongly consider using this service or a similar one.

Facebook ads

For a fee, you can advertise your brand on Facebook, specifying who sees your ad, where in the world the ad is run, and which key words you want to use. Facebook charges either per view (called impression) or per click, and the prices vary depending on how specific you get in your requirements and how many other advertisers are targeting the same market. Facebook enables you to set a daily limit on your advertising spending and offers suggestions for your bid (how much you pay) per click.

Creating your website

You should bear in mind the following key rules when designing your site, from both a financial and an aesthetic perspective:

Website design

Keep your costs as low as possible by learning how to design your own site or employing the services of a technically minded friend or contact.

Website hosting/Dedicated URL

URL stands for "universal resource locator," which is your web address. Do you want to have your brand name as the primary component? If so, search online to see if the URL has already been taken. If it has, be creative by using alternative extensions such as .co, .net, or .biz.

If you want to have a dedicated URL, you need to find hosting. Host companies offer a wide range of services, from "turn-key" (end-to-end) websites (in which they do the design, uploading, hosting, and management of your site for you) to simple hosting, where you are responsible for all aspects of design, uploading, and management.

Website hosting/Shared URL

A more affordable option for hosting your site is to go with a free, online, turn-key website provider. These are website design and hosting companies that offer both free and paid services. Some examples include moonfruit.com and limedomains.com. If you use the free service on these types of providers, your URL can contain your brand name, but it will be under the domain of the provider. For example, if you host on www. babyjane.com (a fictitious hosting provider), your URL may look something like this: http:// audreycouture.babyjane.com. For many start-up designers, the no overhead, pre-designed, easy-to-navigate websites are a good option. However, if your clients enter "audreycouture" in a search engine, your site may not show up, as it is the subdomain of the primary domain babyjane.com.

Blogs

With blogging software (such as wordpress.com and blogger.com), you can set up your own blog/website with relative ease; they offer a multitude of different templates for your blog and can enable additional customization. Blogs offer you two ways to host your page, either for free or for a fee. There are pros and cons to both, and it is important that you evaluate your needs—as well as your budget— before launching your blog. One important point when considering blogs is the fact that they are more often used by industry observers, as opposed to designers themselves.

Checklist: Developing a web presence

- Have you planned to make the most of the virtual world?
- Do your websites encourage viewer participation and loyalty?
- Do you have the skills to design and develop your own website?

- Is a dedicated or shared URL more suitable for your purposes?
- Have you explored the advantages of using blogging?

- Have you looked into the effectiveness of using search engines?
- Have you considered advertising your brand on social networking sites?

- Are you fully exploiting the benefits of social networking?

Structure and order

• KEY RULES FOR STRUCTURING AN EFFECTIVE PORTFOLIO
• UNDERSTANDING WHAT TO INCLUDE IN A GRADUATE PORTFOLIO

The key goals when creating a portfolio are to convey a strong sense of identity and to showcase your talents in a unique way.

Although it is important for your unique talents to be adequately showcased, following a simple outline in terms of content will ensure that basic expectations have been met. In general, interviewers want to see evidence of creative and technical knowledge, strong professional abilities, and a unique, creative point of view. In addition, you will need to stand out in this hyper-competitive profession by flaunting work that surpasses scores of previous applicants in these areas, while showing a stellar presentation that the interviewer will remember. Perhaps the greatest mistake is to create a book that lacks creative soul and blends in with all the other books simply because the presentation lacked originality.

◀▶ REINVENTING THE LAYOUT
There is no rule for how you lay out your figures in your final presentation. Avoid predictability, vary the figure styling, alter your mediums, and flaunt your abilities through drawing, digital, and other skills you possess.

Checklist: Content

- Does your portfolio meet the basic content criteria?
- Have you demonstrated creative and technical knowledge?
- Is your portfolio highly original and creative?

- Will your portfolio help you stand out among other graduates?
- Have you followed the "less is more" rule and included only your strongest work?

- Do the contents of your portfolio leave the audience eager to see more of your work?
- Have you asked for constructive criticism of your portfolio?
- Is your portfolio forward-thinking?

- Does your portfolio address a variety of seasons, colors, and fabric stories?
- Do you need a separate croquis book?
- Have you identified three to four external groups?

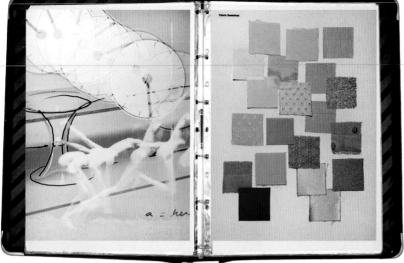

Introduce your inspiration and fabrics to connect
with your viewer

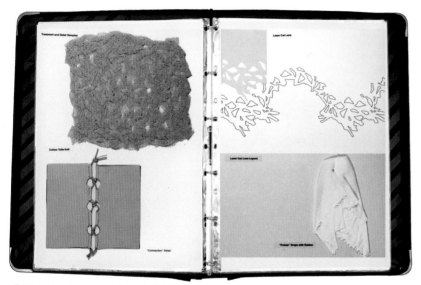

Fabric treatments, sewn samples, and prints flaunt
skills and convey design details

Figures and flats may be shown on separate layouts
or alongside each other

5 rules for structuring a portfolio

1 Be memorable
Stand out from scores of applicants by showing work that breaks the mold on what a portfolio can showcase. For some, this may mean a separate croquis book and portfolio, whereas others might create one book that is a combination of the two. In either case, demonstrating an exciting and unique presentation style and design aesthetic is critical.

2 Don't overload
You will have spent large amounts of time, creativity, and emotion producing your work, but show only your best work, even if this means reducing the quantity of work so that the collective whole appears stronger.

3 Never leave them satiated
Always leave your audience curious to see more. A portfolio that makes your audience hungry for more is more memorable than one that is too full of work and saturated with information.

4 The external editor
Gaining insight to your portfolio from a well-trained, objective eye is critical when curating your groups. Although faculty is a great resource, seek feedback from a professional designer, head hunter, or other fashion professional, who will view your work objectively. Acting on constructive criticism will enable you to make improvements before the interview stage.

5 Remember, there are no real rules
Fashion is about breaking the mold, predicting the future, and offering what's new. Look at the great designers of history, and consider how they challenged the world's perceptions of fashion design and went against the grain. Dior rebelled with his "New Look," Prada offered clean simplicity in an era of ostentation and logo-mania, and Donna Karan addressed a design niche during the 1980s.

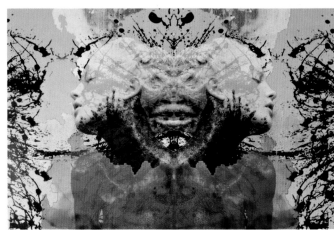

▲▶ AESTHETIC INTRODUCTIONS
Your book and its introductory page ease your viewer into your creative tastes. Like those shown here, you must provide a sense of your aesthetic, which speaks closely to your designs.

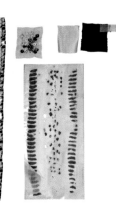

▲▶ FLAUNTING DIVERSITY
Consider the ways you can flaunt your abilities to create diverse color, inspiration, and fabric stories. This resort group successfully addresses concept and motif while adhering to the category through easy-to-travel jersey knits and chiffons.

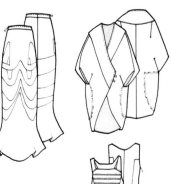

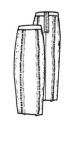

▲▶ COMPOSITION AND SHIFTS
Always create dynamic negative space when composing your flats. Provide the highest degree of design accuracy, and shift your front and back flats up and/or down to give visual depth. Spacing should be consistent between all the flats.

The 6-point portfolio checklist

Viewers will want to see a quantity of work that is diverse yet focused in terms of aesthetic and targeted customer. By addressing a variety of seasons, color, fabric stories, and categories of design, your book will demonstrate your abilities in highly creative ways.

Consider the following framework for your portfolio, particularly if you are seeking your first job. When you are interviewing for positions later in your career, the formula will shift to highlight not only the more specific market you are working in, but also the professional work you have done:

1 The introductory page

The first page introduces a mood, aesthetic, and identity. Like the door to a designer's boutique, it eases the viewer into your creative world. A photograph you've taken, a piece of fine art, your logo, or even a fashion illustration that reflects the attitude of your customer are just some examples of what this page might be.

2 The groupings
Three fall/winter groups

The fall/winter groupings are often ordered as career wear, sportswear, and "a third group" (such as denim, knitwear, or evening wear). As you consider these groupings, solve color and fabric questions in different ways. Career wear may rely on a camel-navy-white story that is graphic in feeling, neat and tailored, and allows looks to be sold "head to toe." Sportswear may feature tonal colors in order to focus on interesting silhouettes and textures, and allow pieces to be "item-driven." The "third group" might include items such as knitwear textures, the denim market (in which attention to detail and fabrication are often the focus), or evening wear that will contain a dramatic resolution.

The pause

Between the core groupings there should be a pause for viewers before they start on another large core body of work. Possibilities include accessories, a resort or holiday group that is delivered to stores after the fall deliveries, or a group that is experimental and flaunts your creative abilities.

Three spring/summer groups

Similar to the fall/winter core, this area addresses three groupings. These are a career wear section; a relaxed sportswear grouping that focuses more heavily on silhouette, detail, and item; and a final group that targets activewear, evening wear, or knitwear. This will round out the core by supplying diverse color, fabric, and silhouette development.

3 The croquis book

Perhaps the most important piece of collateral you can show is your croquis book, which exposes your design processes and true abilities. Your croquis book will probably be the most scrutinized element at an interview. For this reason, consider how it may be used to showcase your design development and sketches, final illustrated groups, fabric samples and swatches, flats, and other design criteria (rather than producing a separate and more formal portfolio). If you only show one book, it must display the same high levels of professional quality and quantity that the separate presentations would contain. Whichever route you decide to take, a highly personalized presentation style is mandatory.

4 The auxiliary portfolio

Occasionally, a separate auxiliary portfolio is needed to highlight special skills, awards, press, or other types of projects. In such cases, this separate portfolio may be shown after the primary portfolio. Remember, everything you show should represent you and, like your primary book, this secondary portfolio must be of the same quality or you may jeopardize your chances of employment. Some designers use this portfolio to show design work that is more conceptual in nature in an effort to highlight their versatility and creative abilities.

5 The press piece

After every interview, provide the interviewer with a reminder of you and your work. This may include your résumé, look book, or a CD of your work. Remember, less is more, so do not overwhelm your viewer. Also include your name, address, email, and website address (if applicable) on a standard-sized sheet of paper.

6 Three to four external groups

External to your portfolio are three to four groups that can be rotated in and out to best target the company that is interviewing you. By carefully considering the categories, fabrications, and color stories for these additional groups, your portfolio will convey a different context when the groups are rearranged.

▼ WELCOME TO YOUR WORLD
An introductory page introduces your viewer to the creative world that you inhabit. This abstract page still suggests mood, customer, silhouette, and what's to come.

Targeting your portfolio

- **IDENTIFY YOUR TARGET CATEGORIES**
- **IDENTIFY YOUR KEY FASHION HOUSES**

Addressing a highly specific customer ensures that your work conveys confidence and knowledge.

Working on your final collection (see Chapter 1) should help you decide how best to show the area of design that you excel in and also which you wish to pursue professionally. For some, a focused evening wear portfolio that contains a breadth of color and fabric palettes, concepts and inspirations, and approaches to the category is all that is necessary to provide the viewer with enough evidence of talent and skill. Other portfolios may contain a range of sportswear, accessories, evening wear, and other categories to demonstrate a particular aesthetic and house the designer may wish to work for. Whichever you decide, you must always consider which houses you intend to interview with before you begin your book's individual groups.

◀ START WITH STYLE
The reinterpretation of familiar, youthful silhouettes gives this collection a lighthearted attitude. Modern colors, fabric choices, and reimagined proportions ensure the designs remain forward-thinking and relevant.

Checklist: How to target your portfolio

- Have you examined the area of fashion in which you are most likely to succeed?
- Are you focusing on one price point?
- Are you still maintaining your creative integrity?
- Have you clearly identified your target customer?
- Will the fabrics, colors, inspirations, and other items confuse your target customer?
- Have you covered a range of seasons and categories?
- Have you considered which are the key companies that you wish to target?
- Are you performing adequate research on the shop floor?

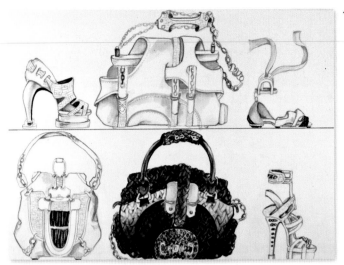

◄▼ ADDRESS ALL AREAS
Although a portfolio may be geared toward a particular area, the inclusion of other categories will flaunt your versatility, talent, and aesthetic focus. As a recent graduate, showing diverse design abilities is critical for garnering your first job.

The targeting checklist

Use the following points to help identify your target category or categories:

One price point
Whether you showcase one focused category such as accessories or several to convey a particular lifestyle and aesthetic, your groups must all adhere to one price point. Do you wish to interview for Abercrombie & Fitch or Carolina Herrera? Fabrics, details, construction techniques, and even how the styling is handled must all be a part of the same family. Remember, however, that creativity is what matters most, regardless of market or category.

A clearly defined customer
Similar to price point, the customer you target must be specific within the book. Diversify colors, fabrics, inspirations, and items to flaunt your versatility, but do not confuse your viewer by offering collections that conflict in aesthetic or usability. Consider what your customers need from fashion and what they may wish their wardrobes to communicate about them. By listing such adjectives, you will form a base on which to design each grouping. Do they want fashion that is familiar in silhouette, yet unique in fabric development or color usage (as shown at Miu Miu and Prada)?

Do they look for garments that question conventional fashion by employing unusual silhouette and construction, such as the fashion of Comme des Garçons?

A range of seasons
Most designers create collections that address not only seasons, but also categories. Fall/winter, spring/summer and resort/vacation are the commonly shown collections designers create each year. To demonstrate your understanding of seasonal dressing, fabric types, methods for styling, color usage, and how your vision will adjust because of such factors, you must include a range of seasons within your portfolio. Consider how the groups may address variations within each season.

Five to seven key companies
Before you begin your portfolio, consider five to seven companies that you wish to target. By listing companies that have similar price points, customer bases, views of today's fashion, and even color and fabric sensibilities, you are more likely to fit in with their design team. Always strive to be five steps ahead,

so that you give them what's new and exciting (without making the work irrelevant to the house).

Shopping reports
There's no better way to learn about fashion than from the retail experience. When you visit the sales floor, take note of what is on sale and what is selling well. Then, learn from the sales help because they engage with those who matter most: customers. Customers are quick to confide in sales help by offering their opinions on a collection in addition to what they need most. This type of research not only will impress your interviewer, but also will help you create a highly relevant portfolio that addresses shifts in consumer behavior. Learning this skill early will allow you to segue into the professional world more seamlessly, because all designers perform such research throughout their career.

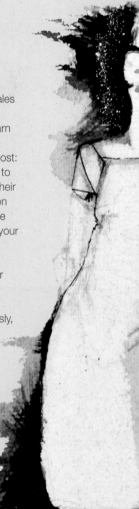

Targeting your portfolio:
Women's sportswear

- **THE KEY HALLMARKS OF SPORTSWEAR COLLECTIONS**
- **HOW TO VARY DESIGN INTENSITIES**

Sportswear designers create a full wardrobe for their customers through well-merchandised looks that contain an array of fabrications and items.

▼► FULL CIRCLE
The transition from vertical tailored looks, through more item-driven sportswear that moves the eye horizontally, to elongated evening looks is successfully shown in this collection. The recurring use of line as motif that is the transition from structure (vertical order), to fracture (diagonal movement) and back to vertical structure, is also demonstrated in silhouettes that move from flat to draped.

As perhaps the largest category of fashion design, sportswear relates to virtually everyone regardless of demographic and psychographic. The sportswear concept of mix-and-match clothing provides customers with "one-stop shopping" in which every need is met and items range in design intensity. From the familiar silhouettes of a tailored jacket and trench coat to more elaborate creations such as a sculptural dress for special occasions, the sportswear customer can fulfill all his or her needs within the collection.

When you design your collection, always work from the top down, starting with the top 20 percent of intensity (see "Varying design intensities," opposite).

5 hallmarks of a sportswear collection

1 Contains a cohesive, well-structured fabric story with woven and knitted fabrics in varying weights and textures.

2 Consists of mix-and-match wardrobe, containing outerwear, jackets, tops, bottoms, and dresses.

3 Provides the customer with "one-stop shopping" through well-formulated merchandising.

4 Contains varying degrees of design intensity to provide the customer with diverse experiences.

5 Displays a clear and consistent point of view that is unique to the designer throughout the looks.

Varying design intensities

The levels of design should vary within your collection. By segmenting the collection into three areas in this way, you not only address all of your customer's needs, but also create broader price points within the collection. You will also produce a highly contextualized body of work.

The top 20 percent are those items that are extreme representations of your collection's concept and inspiration. They may be showpieces strictly relegated to the runway and not for sale, or those that are very expensive and not made in high quantities. For example, Oscar de la Renta may create an expensive embroidered coat that only a few stores will purchase, whereas Viktor and Rolf's showpieces serve merely to create media buzz and provide evidence of their dramatic concepts.

The middle 60 percent is the core and contains work that retailers and customers will identify as the hallmarks of the collection. This area still contains levels of design intensity and requires the most strategic development in order to attract vast quantities of retailers, editors, and customers. The area contains such familiar silhouettes as the tailored jacket that may have an interesting detail, along with those pieces that are filtered down from the more extreme top 20 percent.

The bottom 20 percent includes those pieces that, without the context of the entire collection, could appear somewhat generic. A traditional black suit, a crisp tailored shirt, and even the iconic T-shirt are all items made from the collection's fabrications and provide a customer with less involved, "quieter" pieces. This section also allows non-core customers to be a part of the designer's world through less costly pieces.

**Top 20%:
High concept**
The extreme silhouette and fabrication immediately convey the design concept.

20%

60%

20%

Middle 60%: Core identity
Wearable, yet highly original pieces are adapted from the top. This field must also contain varying design intensities.

**Bottom 20%:
Simple filtrations**
Simplified silhouettes are developed using the collection's fabrics and details.

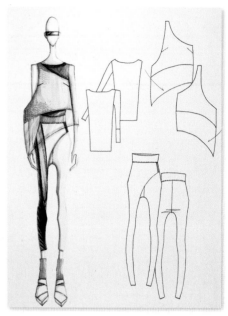

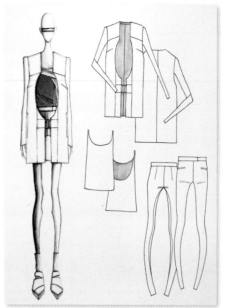

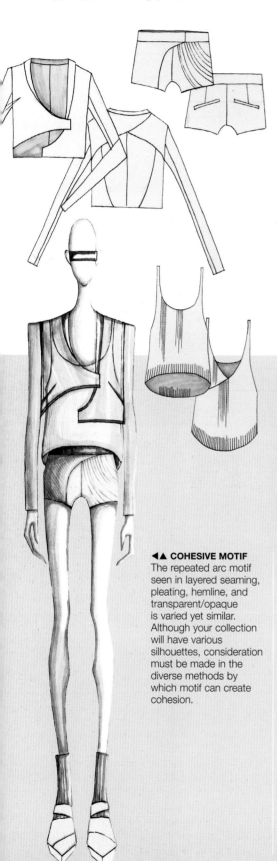

◄▲ COHESIVE MOTIF
The repeated arc motif seen in layered seaming, pleating, hemline, and transparent/opaque is varied yet similar. Although your collection will have various silhouettes, consideration must be made in the diverse methods by which motif can create cohesion.

Sportswear merchandising:
Groups of six or seven looks

Although there is no set formula for what designers offer their audience each season, a simple guideline for sportswear collections will provide a framework from which you can divert, depending on your own vision and customer's needs. This template gives each collection breadth and context, while also ensuring that fabric and color palettes are successfully resolved. A collection of six or seven looks in the portfolio typically contains:

Three or four outerwear options
Regardless of the season and climate, every collection must contain outerwear. Even during the summer, your customer may need an item for cool days, or protection from the sun and rain. Most collections offer one tailored option, one shorter option, and a novelty version in an interesting fabric or silhouette. As with the varying levels of design, each outerwear option should give your customer a different experience and occasion.

Two to four jackets
Not every designer will offer a traditionally tailored jacket, but all must address this category. The jacket may be part of a suit where fabrics match, a jacket that is cut in a novelty fabric worn with an alternate fabric bottom, and even

thin leathers or nylon for dramatic textural contrast. Solids, prints, and even hand-painted fabrics may be appropriate for your customer. Depending upon the climate, this item might also serve as an outerwear item.

Two or three shirts/blouses
As a layering device or an item that stands alone because of its interesting design, this item addresses virtually every occasion and customer type. Such examples include the classic man's-style shirt in crisp cotton; the floral, printed, sheer cotton voile tunic; the metallic, charmeuse halter-neck top that goes from day to night; and the sculptural, embroidered, or beaded top that demands its own spotlight.

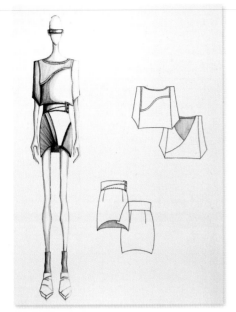

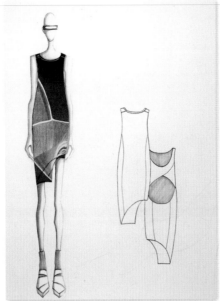

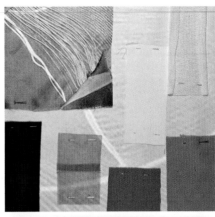

Two to four knits

Knitwear is essential in every sportswear collection and can include sheer cashmere knits, iconic cut-and-sew shirts, jersey T-shirts, and highly dense knitwear that can serve as outerwear. Like the shirting category, items may serve as devices for layering and color accents or as pieces that are true works of art, such as those designed by Sandra Backlund. A variety of fiber types, machine-knit and cut-and-sew, solids with graphic designs, and category types must all be considered. Consider how knitwear could be used as evening wear; how print, appliqué, or beading could create dynamic results; and even how knitwear could be used in such nonconventional ways as the tailored jacket or accessories.

Two or three pants

Pants allow for a wide variety of silhouette directions within a collection. From the strictly tailored and cuffed trouser that may be part of a suiting look to the slouchy denim or cotton twill pant that gives movement and a relaxed mood, pants come in all shapes and fabrications. They generally remain quieter in detail in order to support the top's more considered design, although

this is not always the case, particularly in the denim market, where detail, top-stitching, grommets, and pockets give the category its signature.

Two or three skirts

Similar to pants, skirts form an integral part of a collection's merchandising and must offer your customer a variety of silhouettes, fabrications, and experiences. However, designers are often more experimental with skirt silhouettes and fabric choices because of the broader range of lengths and occasions at which skirts are worn. Such extremities include a strictly tailored pencil skirt in wool gabardine; a sculpturally draped bubble skirt in duchesse satin; a billowy, printed, chiffon, floor-length silhouette; an embroidered, tiered peasant skirt; and a caviar-beaded miniskirt for evening.

One or two dresses

Dresses have become increasingly popular because of the ease of choice they offer when dressing, and the way in which they elongate the silhouette. Depending on the customer's way of life, dresses can be for work, play, evening, and city or country lifestyles, and used as either a layering or statement piece.

▲ **PERFECT PAIRINGS**
When working with color palettes, designers often provide their customer with diverse color percentages. This collection allows the wearer to choose predominantly lighter or darker looks, along with more balanced pairings.

Solids or prints, familiar silhouettes or architectural confections, and designed with modesty or seduction in mind, dresses are the ultimate blank canvas. When you show dresses in your collection, offer a diversity of fabrics along with pieces that merely serve as a backdrop to others or as an element that adds drama to the collection's context.

Checklist: Build a winning sportswear portfolio

- Do fabric stories include wovens and knits?

- Are solids and prints shown?

- How cohesive and well rounded are the groupings? Is there repetition?

- Do collections allow enough variety in color, design, and occasion?

- How has the 20/60/20 percent ratio been addressed?

- Are there any items that seem inconsistent with the customer's lifestyle?

- Where do fabric treatment samples need to be provided for clarity?

- Is the quality of the work consistent throughout the portfolio?

- Do some areas need more visual articulation for clarity?

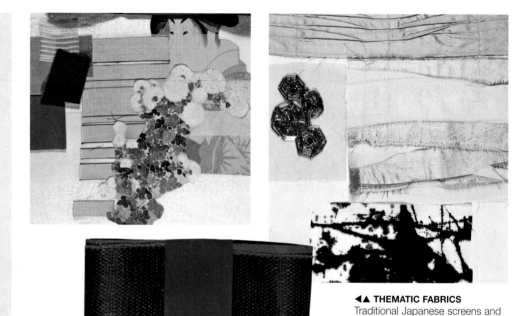

◀▲ THEMATIC FABRICS
Traditional Japanese screens and garment construction provide this collection with great clarity. Wood-blocked fabrics, sheer stripes created by pulled threads, and organic pleating all reference the cultural theme while offering the consumer with a diversity of item, treatment, silhouette, and occasion.

▼▶ A FULL LIFESTYLE
Sportswear designers rely on their well-honed understanding of their customer when creating collections. All types of item and occasion must be addressed in order to supply the customer with a wardrobe filled with core basics and novelty statement pieces.

Targeting your portfolio:
Women's evening wear

- **THE ROLE OF SILHOUETTE AND FABRICATION**
- **USING COLOR EFFECTIVELY**

From the world of red-carpet gowns to casual dinners requiring separates, the evening wear portfolio should address every evening event.

Groupings in the evening wear category must provide the customer with a variety of experiences, fabrications, and occasions. The narrower a portfolio's targeted category, the more diverse the groupings must be. Portfolios dedicated exclusively to categories such as evening wear, bridal, lingerie, and accessories need to fully present the various design approaches associated with their particular niche. For evening wear, the portfolio must demonstrate the full spectrum of soft and tailored dressing, dresses and separates, woven fabrics and knitwear, solids and prints, and plain fabrics and embellishments. By imagining the

▼▶ FOR ALL OCCASIONS
Evening wear is much more than red-carpet couture gowns. Separates, day-to-night silhouettes, and less ornate options should be included in your book to demonstrate your market awareness and aesthetic versatility.

Traditional evening wear and sportswear fabrics are mixed for a young, modern customer.

Evening jackets provide this collection with full merchandising.

Checklist: Build a winning evening wear portfolio

- Are diverse approaches to evening wear demonstrated?
- Do fabrications address the notion and aesthetic of evening wear for your customer?
- Is a mixture of both soft and tailored design provided?

- Is a range of both casual and red-carpet classifications covered?
- Are fabric samples (beading, embroidery, and so on) provided to clearly articulate design intention?

- How well do the groupings address the current market and forecast future changes in evening wear?
- Are silhouettes and hemlines varied throughout your portfolio?

- Are dresses and separates offered? Wovens and knitwear?
- How defined is your customer's age range? Is this a factor for your customer?

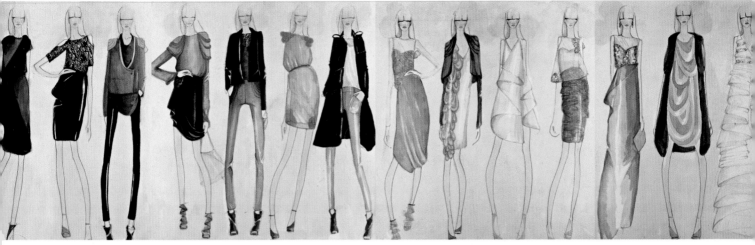

▲▶ FULL RANGE
A fully merchandised evening collection uses the same principles as sportswear. Transitions of color, various silhouettes, cohesive motif, and a strong narrative arc provide one-stop shopping.

types of events at which your customer may wear a late-day ensemble, you will easily be able to identify and diversify fabrications, silhouettes, inspirations, and research.

Although your targeted customer may not buy all of your evening looks, you must still analyze the groupings as you would a traditional sportswear portfolio through a well-considered merchandising plan. Do you have variations of length? Do the collections utilize various fabric weights and treatments? Are dresses and separates offered? Do categories cover red-carpet events all the way down to an intimate dinner at the local bistro? Like any well-merchandised collection, the customer must be provided with a variety of fashion and clothing experiences within the portfolio.

Silhouette and fabrication

Silhouette and fabrication deserve particular experimentation in evening wear. As the category and time of day are so specific, diversity in these two areas will allow groupings to stand on their own and avoid a redundancy of design approach. For instance, although a designer's approach may be very sculptural, allowances must be made through design versatility for a slightly broader customer base. For many designers, this simply entails reformulating some of their signature motifs and shapes into fabrications that will convey a different feeling. Stiff, sculptural silhouettes, for example, may be rethought and cut in silk chiffon or matte jersey. Although the details may remain, the clothing experience has radically changed in an effort to strengthen merchandising and increase the customer base.

Fabric selections can also greatly enhance your portfolio's diversity. Although some designers, such as Reem Acra, adhere to conventional evening wear fabrics and silhouettes, others prefer to challenge our notion of the category through their fusion of form

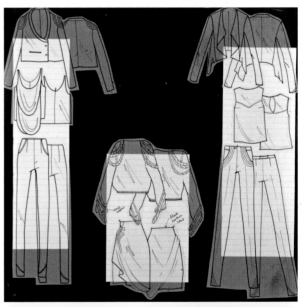

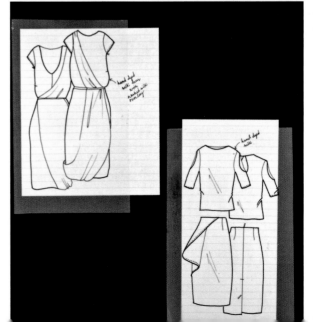

and fabrication, such as DKNY's iconic neoprene ball gowns. How can traditional evening wear fabrics be synthesized with sportswear silhouettes such as a trench coat in duchesse satin? How could a traditional evening wear silhouette, such as a strapless column, be rethought in an unconventional fabric such as denim or embroidered cotton poplin?

Architects and decorators: The difference

Within the seemingly limitless aesthetics offered by fashion design, two types of designer often appear. Consider evening wear and how it has been approached throughout history. Designers such as Yohji Yamamoto, Charles James, Balenciaga, and Vionnet often rely on simple fabric to support experimentations of form, drape, and architectural construction. Conversely, designers who focus on print design, beading, fabric treatment, or other forms of surface embellishment often select silhouettes that support their textile decoration. As a designer, it is essential not to let the two focuses compete for attention. A colorful, heavily beaded fabric may best be shown on a simple, strapless evening gown, whereas a plain, black, silk faille will provide the blank canvas for a sculptural design focus.

Coloring your emotions

In every fashion market and category, a consideration of color (and noncolor) is critical in order to address your customer and the collection's mood accurately. Proportions of color, placement,

◄ **FORM AND SURFACE**
The diverse approach to design is demonstrated in these two groups. Whereas one (top left) uses simple fabric to allow drape and form and make a statement, the other (left) employs a familiar silhouette to showcase extreme textile wizardry.

Choosing colors: The artist as inspiration

Looking at work by reputable artists past and present will help you to understand the connection between color and emotion. When viewing a painting, ask yourself the following questions:

• What is the scale of color and how does this elicit emotion?

• How would another palette change the subject's mood?

• What is the artist trying to communicate through color? With color shapes?

• How would the mood change if the paint were applied differently? More controlled? More gestural?

• Would your emotions change if the artwork were twice as large or twice as small? Why?

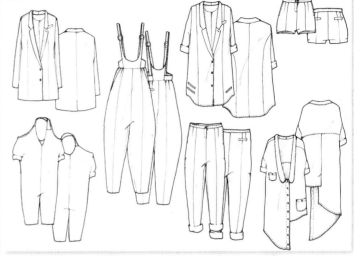

◀▲ DRESSED-DOWN DRESS UP
An evening wear portfolio must address a range of silhouettes and events for the customer's experience. Groupings such as this collection composed primarily of casual silhouettes cut in evening fabrics balance more traditional forms of red-carpet dresses.

fabrication employed, and, of course, the color's tone all play vital roles in the intended message. For example, how would you describe the customer wearing layers of gray shades and dusty mauve and the customer wearing contrast colors of white, tomato-red, denim-blue, and black? The calming, vertical silhouette created through sophisticated tonal relationships often appears more mature as opposed to the energetic, horizontally blocked figure that uses sharp contrasts to achieve a more youthful feeling. This is an important consideration in the evening wear category, in which women often wear color in bolder and more interesting ways. From long, red, chiffon columns to vibrantly printed and beaded cocktail dresses, experimentation with color can be a dramatic focus in a collection.

When considering how color relationships can elicit different emotions, research art history. Color is used in a highly foundational manner to support both mood and subject. From the extreme color proportions of Barnett Newman's abstract canvases to the tonal sensitivity and intimate scales of Monet's haystack series, artists choose wisely to give profoundly different experiences.

Once you gain an understanding of how color relationships and usages, and not just the colors themselves, can address a mood and customer, start to view runway shows. How has the designer used color to move your eye? How does this make you feel about the work? How would the collection change if it were re-colored more tonally or more graphically? Do the silhouettes and design aesthetic change meaning?

Lingerie and loungewear

- **LEARN ABOUT THE MAIN LINGERIE CATEGORIES**
- **DISCOVER THE WIDE VARIETY OF LINGERIE PRODUCTS**

There are few sartorial luxuries that can beat beautifully crafted lingerie. What was once largely hidden from view and simply made is now a creative force in fashion design, and your lingerie portfolio should reflect this in an organized and dynamic manner.

Today's lingerie and loungewear markets encompass a wide range of items because of the modern-day consumer's increasing need for well-designed fashion, advances in fabric technology, and the passing of various social rules. From the creation of spandex by DuPont in 1959 to the charmeuse and chiffon beaded camisole that takes the wearer from day to night, the contemporary market receives as much design attention as runway fashion design. As a lingerie designer, you must utilize a core understanding of design principles for every collection you propose, including customer targeting, inspiration research, color and fabric development, use of motif, and merchandising for one-stop shopping.

Categories of design

Lingerie is usually divided into three categories: foundation wear, underwear, and sleepwear. Foundation wear garments include bras, corsets, waspies, and basques, which typically require bra cups and other forms of understructure. Underwear includes less structured items such as panties, camisoles, and slips. As the title suggests, sleepwear consists of soft-dressing items such as pajamas, robes, nightgowns, and negligees.

Although they may appear to be separate from the lingerie category, swimwear, beachwear, and dancewear are often included in this area, and you should consider adding them to your portfolio. Fabrications, cup construction, and silhouettes are similar, and some fashion brands cater to all four!

▲ **ROMANTIC DESIRES**
Well-crafted lingerie exemplifies what fashion is all about: it surpasses mere utilitarian need and fulfills aesthetic and emotional desire.

◄ **INTIMATE LUXURIES**
High-end lingerie houses use couture-quality laces, silks, and construction techniques. Runway shows, such as La Perla's seen here, position a brand within the fashion elite.

Checklist: Build a winning lingerie portfolio

- Have you utilized customer targeting, inspiration research, color and fabric development, and motif in your lingerie portfolio?
- Have you created a one-stop shopping experience for the customer?

- Have you considered the key areas of lingerie and loungewear?
- Does your collection offer a full spectrum of lingerie products?

- Does your portfolio reflect how lingerie may be worn out of context (perhaps as formal evening wear)?
- Have you researched top brands to increase your technical knowledge?

- Are you keeping updated on current trends within the lingerie market?
- Do you understand what qualities create a sought-after lingerie item?

▲ GROUNDING BLOCKS
The fabrications, items, and silhouette varieties in lingerie are limited. As a result, designers rely on interesting color and texture combinations to complement technical construction.

Parameters that challenge creativity
You should approach lingerie design in a similar way to accessory design. An exceptional attention to detail is critical for success, as is an enjoyment of working with specific fabric types such as silks, laces, and mesh. Unlike in sportswear, fabric choices are restricted by narrower market preferences, whereas innovative silhouette development is less diverse. However, lingerie designers usually enjoy the challenge of working within confined design parameters to create exciting new collections. If that is you, then you are perfect for this specialty!

Not just undergarments
Before the invention of stretch fabrics, undergarments were made from woven linen and cotton. With moldable fabrics making complex construction a thing of the past, undergarments have come into their own luxury category. From Gaultier's cone-bra worn by Madonna during her 1990 "Blond Ambition" tour to La Perla's undergarments that might easily be worn for an opening night at La Scala, designers have referenced lingerie with highly creative results.

In today's lingerie market, this blurring of categories is particularly relevant. Although your portfolio will encompass underwear to be worn under garments, the day-to-night category must also be addressed in order to demonstrate your creative breadth. Lace bodysuits, jeweled camisoles, embroidered satin corsets, and negligees that also serve as formal evening wear are just some of the design areas your portfolio can include.

The top lingerie fashion houses

Increase your creative and technical knowledge by researching top brands. This will not only keep you updated about trends and shifts in consumer behavior, but it will also help you to learn what makes a top product. High-quality fabrics, interesting design, superior fit, and innovative details lead to repeat customers and can create a globally renowned brand. Listed below are some of the leading houses in the lingerie market:

- La Perla
- Agent Provocateur
- Natori
- Victoria's Secret
- Chantelle
- Lise Charmel
- Triumph
- Spoylt
- Eres
- Hanro
- Laurela
- Allure de Star
- Damaris
- Fogal
- Aubade

Providing a full spectrum

Offering a diversity of products will demonstrate both your knowledge of and your passion for this category, as well as your ability to design virtually anything for the lingerie market. Listed below are those items included in every lingerie portfolio.

Foundation wear
Corsets
Corselettes
Basques
Bustiers
Waspies

Underwear
Bras
Briefs and panties
Thongs
French knickers
Cami-knickers
Camisoles
Slips

Sleepwear
Nightdresses
Nightshirts
Pajamas
Dressing gowns
Bathrobes
Negligees
Kimonos

Swimwear and other
One-piece swimsuits
Bikinis
Tankinis
Strapless suits
Bodysuits
Leotards
Beach wraps
Kaftans
Jumpsuits
Playsuits

Targeting your portfolio:
Men's sportswear

- **THE KEY ATTRIBUTES OF A MENSWEAR DESIGNER**
- **MENSWEAR AS AN EXCITING DESIGN AREA**

With male consumers paying more attention to fashion, there is a growing demand for new talent in this design category.

▲ PROPORTION AND DETAIL
Menswear relies heavily upon reworked proportion and detail development. The shrunken blazer, elongated knitted cardigan, and classic white shirt are given a fresh twist here when contextualized with more conventional silhouettes.

Despite its seemingly limited format for design development, menswear is perhaps the most creatively challenging of all the markets. Silhouettes rarely deviate from the familiar, design evolution is comparatively slow, fabrications and color palettes are less varied, and the market's exposure is smaller.

Finding ways to innovate this category within such tight parameters can make men's sportswear hugely enjoyable for many designers. For example, consider how you could update the basic white shirt. Although the silhouette and construction may be similar to those of the previous season, the subtlety of detail, fabric choice, collection's context, and even button trim can all have great impact in the market. Similarly, the menswear market contains less diversities and extremities of customer than the womenswear market; fabrications, textures, and silhouette are often based on familiar elements that slowly morph over time through subtle change. For these reasons, menswear often attracts those who have an exceptional sensitivity to line, shape, color, and detail rather than those who wish to reinvent design with each new season.

Checklist: Build a winning menswear portfolio

- Are details highly developed and visually clear?
- Are fabric samples used to convey detail?
- Do fabrications adhere to the customer's lifestyle?
- Are designs innovative while adhering to the framework of menswear?

- Is color usage appropriate for menswear?
- Do the textures, treatments, and details relate to the concept and inspiration?
- How mix-and-match are the items?
- How do the groups relate in mood and design? Are they targeting the same customer?

- Does your customer appreciate more overt detail, subtle detail, or a balance of both?
- How adventurous is your customer when it comes to silhouette? Can items challenge preconceived notions, or must they always be considered within a traditional template?

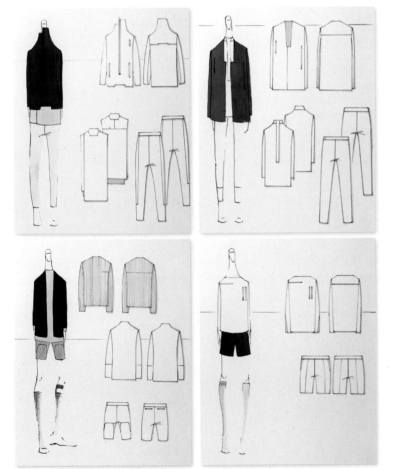

◀▼ MAXIMUM MINIMALISM

Fashion is an extreme representation of an idea and aesthetic, no matter what the resource. Despite appearing "undesigned," this collection relies on bold, clean graphic shapes with well-considered line and proportion. When choosing an illustration style, analyze how the figure, choice of medium, and composition can accentuate your collection's extreme element.

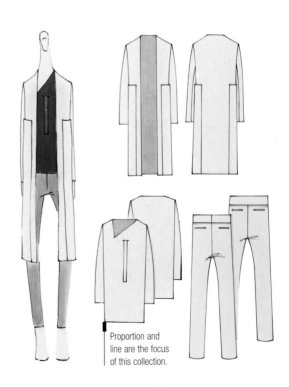

Proportion and line are the focus of this collection.

7 key attributes of a menswear designer

Menswear can be a tremendously rewarding area for the right type of designer. Listed below are some characteristics commonly associated with designers in this market:

1 Supportive fabrics and colors
The majority of menswear designers base their collections on traditional, menswear-type fabrics and colors, while accenting this core with novelties. Although silhouettes and proportions may swerve subtly from the norm over time, rarely will the male customer respond to fabrications and color palettes that do not appear masculine or familiar. For example, most won't respond to such fabrics as chiffon, charmeuse, Lurex, or lace (which are commonly relegated to womenswear) or to color stories that appear feminine.

2 It's all in the details
Detail development is one of the primary foundations in menswear design. The contrasting color of a shirt collar, a new pocket design and proportion, innovative top-stitching, contrast seam-binding inside an unlined jacket, or the new silhouette of a pleated pant are just some examples of how the menswear market suggests new design to its customers. Although some designers, such as Paul Smith and Thom Browne, utilize iconic menswear details, others develop their own innovations, such as those seen at Neil Barrett and Raf Simons.

3 Familiar silhouettes
Since the creation of the modern suit in the nineteenth century, menswear has typically developed from existing silhouettes. Some of these have been born from utilitarian need, including the trench coat and safari jacket, whereas others have served as statement pieces such as the leather biker jacket. However, the general garment silhouettes in today's menswear have remained unchanged because practicality is a high priority for most male customers. Menswear adheres to familiar blocks each season and then updates them through detail and technology.

4 The merchandising formula
Because silhouette experimentation is less prominent in menswear, the merchandising formula is stricter. The typical, fashion-forward, male consumer desires a wardrobe that is updated and interesting, yet easy to wear and does not reinvent conventional silhouettes. The trench coat, the tailored jacket, the men's shirt, flat-front or pleated pants, the T-shirt, and sweater knits are just some of the essential components in every menswear collection. Whereas womenswear may seek to abstract such items through a sculptural approach or even practicality, menswear will always offer less divergence from familiar silhouettes when merchandised. Similarly, the male customer rarely looks to the designer for head-to-toe looks, which results in a greater need for mix-and-match merchandise.

5 Interpretations of a theme
How a collection is developed from an inspiration or theme is often less literal for menswear. Consider the historically based creations of the late Alexander McQueen and the fantasies of Galliano and Kawakubo when contrasted with the less overtly influenced collections of Neil Barrett or Lucas Ossendrijver for Lanvin. This underscores a particular approach to menswear, in which inspiration is suggested rather than shown literally in addition to how men want to be perceived in their clothing.

6 Slow evolutions
When Helmut Lang and Hedi Slimane created radically slimmer silhouettes for menswear in the 1990s, a revolution occurred. This shift in proportion would seem insignificant in the fast-paced world of womenswear, but it created a new aesthetic in menswear that had remained unchanged for decades. When viewed over time, the rapidity and acceptability of change in the two markets could not be more different. For this reason, often those who gravitate into menswear are inspired by contemplative and quieter elements of design.

7 The customer base
Where the world of womenswear is seemingly endless in the types of customers and aesthetics addressed, the menswear market is less diverse. Although demographics and psychographics alter from house to house and there is a level of demand for change and newness each season, the approach to menswear is often dictated by lifestyle and seems less nuanced.

◄ **REWORKING PRECONCEPTIONS**
Lanvin menswear frequently appropriates womenswear fabrications into conventional menswear silhouettes in order to update the familiar. Such subtle design shifts reflect a consumer who is less attracted to complicated and sculptural silhouettes.

▶ **NEW-WORLD DETAILS**
Research of indigenous tribes provides ideas for silhouette, detail, and portfolio art direction.

Laced ties repeat as a focused motif.

A unique font on parchment paper supports the group's historical theme.

Clean accessory silhouettes give attitude without competing with the graphic clothing silhouettes.

Men's evening wear

- **THE TUXEDO'S COMPONENTS**
- **TAKING MEN'S EVENING WEAR BEYOND THE TUXEDO**

Although often dominated in the past by the tuxedo, today men's evening wear encompasses a wide range of fashion design possibilities. Your portfolio should offer an updated approach while reflecting your customer's aesthetic preferences.

From the elegant tuxedo to underground club wear, men's evening wear reflects the customer's unique lifestyle and personality. Whereas some men choose the traditional formula, others use creative expression to challenge the status quo. Although women's evening wear displays a tremendous variety of silhouettes, men's evening wear has to be unique in order to differentiate it from the daytime look and experience.

Today's tuxedo

Long held as the de facto choice for evening events, the tuxedo (and all its iterations) is today governed by fewer rules than in the past. The tuxedo today ranges from the highly codified versions often seen at weddings to fashionable expressions that suit the wearer's taste. From Stefano Pilati's mechanic-style tuxedo for Dior to the seemingly endless spectrum of colors and untraditional fabrics cut in the traditional silhouette, the tuxedo remains popular for formal occasions despite the increasing unpopularity of the hat, the

◄► UPDATING A CLASSIC
Despite being the conventional choice in men's formal wear, the tuxedo can be given a twist, with changes in fabrication and proportion.

◀ **ALTERNATIVE ROUTES**
What constitutes men's evening wear is framed
by how your customer wishes to express himself.
Whereas some may choose the classic tuxedo, others
may prefer something more personalized, as seen in this
"creative black tie" look by Yohji Yamamoto.

necktie, the business suit, and other formal attires of the past. Key
characteristics of today's tuxedos include the following:

- Tailored jacket in black or midnight blue with silk facings on a
  shawl collar or peaked lapel; notched lapels may be used and
  are considered less formal. An ivory jacket is common during the
  summer and in warmer climates.
- Trousers in matching fabric with a single satin braid or stripe
  covering the outer seams; no cuffs, belt loops, or pleats.
  Suspenders are used to hold the pants up.
- A cummerbund is a traditional part of the tuxedo, although
  modern versions often forgo this accessory.
- A white dress shirt. The Marcella-style is traditional, but other
  options are available. The most formal versions use shirt studs
  and cuff links, but buttoned shirts are also featured. Cuff links are
  gold or silver and may feature onyx or mother of pearl; double
  links have two sides connected by a rod or chain and are
  considered more formal.
- A bow tie in black silk that
  matches the lapel facings.
  Less formal and more
  whimsical options include
  patterns such as plaids or
  novelty motifs.
- Black socks in silk or fine
  wool.
- The black, patent leather,
  lace-up Oxford shoe. The
  opera pump is suitable for
  more formal affairs.

▶ **OUTSIDE THE BOX**
Alternative evening wear options
can be based on sportswear
silhouettes and appropriated to the
category through fabrics and textures.

3 evening wear design rules

**Today, men's evening wear ranges from the
traditional tuxedo with opera pumps and white tie
to a plain, black, cashmere sweater with tailored
trousers, depending on the event and the customer's
aesthetic. Although some customers hold the
traditional view that evening is the time for women
to shine and men to recede, others demand fashion
that is more expressive and unconventional. When
designing men's evening wear, bear the following
fundamental rules in mind:**

1 Opt for a familiar silhouette
Rarely do men want to wear fashion that strays too
far from conventional silhouettes. The tailored jacket, shirt,
and trousers are core components to menswear. How you
fabricate, adjust proportion, and utilize detail will reflect your
target customer's aesthetic as well as the garment's purpose.

2 It's all in the details
Fabrication and details give clues to a garment's function.
Although the silhouette in menswear may not stray far from the
conventional, special fabrics, details, treatments, and trims will
place an ordinary garment in the evening wear category. How
can shine, texture, and design detail give your customer a
look that stands out from their typical daytime wardrobe?
Like women's evening wear, the male customer looks to his
evening wear to provide a unique experience.

3 The new formal
Evening wear is often about extremes, regardless of gender.
Women desire a fantasy experience of silhouette, color, shine,
fabric, and proportion that is highly atypical of their more practical
daytime wardrobe. With men, the same is true when they don a
tuxedo or reinvent what formal attire means. This is often seen at
the Academy Awards or other celebrity events within the creative
industry, when interpretations are highly personalized. For example,
a tuxedo jacket cut in dark denim and worn with cotton twill cargo
pants and white canvas sneakers is an unorthodox approach to
formal attire.

Checklist: Build a winning men's evening wear portfolio

- Do you show an understanding
  of the traditional approach to
  men's evening wear?

- Have you considered the male
  need for a different clothing
  experience from day to night?

- Does your portfolio address
  the growing demand for
  more unconventional men's
  evening wear?

- Are you still adhering to the
  traditional silhouette favored
  by men?

- Have you included fabric
  choices, details, and trims to
  create striking evening wear?

- Have you looked at how the
  texture of the chosen fabric
  best suits the evening
  wardrobe?

- Are you being as inventive as
  possible in your portfolio, giving
  a choice beyond the traditional
  approach to the tuxedo?

Targeting your portfolio:
Childrenswear

- **THE KEY CHILDREN'S DESIGN CATEGORIES**
- **DEVELOP A SUCCESSFUL CHILDRENSWEAR PORTFOLIO**

An often overlooked area of design, childrenswear has grown exponentially during the last ten years, with high levels of design increasingly in demand. A childrenswear portfolio must display your unique design approach, while being sensitive to a parent's sensibilities.

Where conventional aesthetics once dominated, today's childrenswear is highly creative and diverse. Childrenswear designers are a unique group of people, with a particular approach to silhouette, color, scale, and detail. These designers tend to be fun-loving people who channel their whimsical, childlike selves into the clothing they create. They understand how to excite young minds, what types of texture and depth appeal to children, and which details excite both child and parent. They have a strong understanding of color combinations and intricate and tactile details, and are particularly well skilled in creating highly stylized and thematic collections.

Successful childrenswear designers, however, must also display a practical knowledge of the level of physical development of a child when considering garment construction and usage, as well as the choice of fabrics (which need to be durable). They must also demonstrate a good understanding of safety precautions. Depending on a company's location, there may be strict laws that should be followed when designing clothing for kids, who are apt to pull off and swallow trims that are not secure! Many childrenswear designers start by studying womenswear in their academic careers. However, during their studies, they may have discovered the category for a

▲ FASHIONABLY EARLY
Due to demand for highly designed and personalized products, the infants' market has surged, with new designers catering to parents' whimsical tastes. Function is surpassed in this design, which incorporates bold pattern combinations and theatrical ruffles.

◄ TO BOLDLY GO
Childrenswear color palettes, fabric textures, garment proportions, and design detail are dynamic in order to appear playful. Bold colors, variations of linear motif, and interesting textures give this look its energetic yet relaxed feeling.

► ASPIRATIONAL INFLUENCES
Whereas the silhouettes and themes of more mature fashions may offer initial direction for a childrenswear collection, color palettes, proportions, and details are adjusted for a younger audience.

particular project, which allowed a creative lightbulb to go off. A natural gravitation toward playful color palettes, detail development, the literal translation of whimsical themes, and the small proportions finds its niche when applied to the design spirit of infants, toddlers, boys, and girls.

Key design categories

If you are considering entering the childrenswear market, it is useful to look at its three main categories and how they differ or are similar to each other according to age and aesthetic. This will help to improve the success of your designs. For example, which colors are predominant in the infants category? What can or can't you do in toddler wear? Which themes are most appropriate for each category and gender? How do the child's motor skills and overall development impact on design choices? At what age do children become participating shoppers with their parents? These questions should all be considered when designing for the following categories:

Infants

This category includes infants from birth until around one year (when walking usually begins). Infants in this age group have heads that are one-quarter the size of their bodies, so it is essential that garments can be put on and removed easily using snaps and other practical means. The garments are washed frequently, and particular care is placed on designing within safety regulations. Sizes are typically 3, 6, 9, 12, and 18 months, and/or small, medium, large, and extra large. Because designs are largely adapted to cater to a parent's taste, soft colors and fabrics along with a gentle aesthetic dominate. Consumers often prefer gender-based colors and design choices.

Toddlers

The toddler stage usually commences once walking has begun and continues until age three. As a result of the "rough-and-tumble" lifestyle at this age (plus developing motor skills that make food spills frequent), fabrics need to be durable to withstand frequent laundering. Sizes are typically listed as 2T, 3T, and 4T; the letter "T" stands for "toddler" to distinguish it from the next range in childrenswear, and the numbers usually indicate the toddler's age.

Children

Perhaps the most popular category for students studying design, childrenswear ranges from approximately three to six years old. Children's proportions are different because they have gained in height, whereas their heads are more in proportion with their bodies, and they have slightly protruding bellies. Children explore the world in a far more sophisticated, curious, and assertive manner. Although gender still plays a role in design, there is less rigidity than during the previous years. For example, certain types of stripe layouts and graphic designs may be universal. A particularly popular approach in this category can be seen in labels such as Gap boys, in which adult fabrics and silhouettes are simply shrunk to childlike proportions. Sizes are 4, 5, 6, and 6X for girls and 4, 5, 6, and 7 for boys, and these numerical sizes generally correspond to the child's age. Other size distinctions include slim, regular, and husky.

Trends in childrenswear

Like all areas of design, you must be aware of the latest trends in your market. Given the level of social pressure many children face to fit in, the impact that pop culture has on children's tastes, and the speed at which they outgrow clothing, the desire for the latest fashion can be high for both parent and child.

Trends include physical trends, such as "polka dots are in" or the popularity of a particular color, but they also indicate how consumer behavior is evolving. For example, when sustainability and organic cotton became a consumer demand in the adult fashion market, the childrenswear market responded by doing the same for the eco-conscious parent. This is especially relevant to the infants' market in which parents shun chemicals dyes in favor of a healthier, natural alternative for their sensitive newborn.

Current and future market trends in childrenswear are explored in a host of publications, including *Earnshaw's*, *Vogue Bambini*, *Moda Bambini*, and even *Teen Vogue*, in which the teen market trickles down into girlswear. Collection magazines are published when the new season's looks are presented and offer exposure to both the European and American markets. Not unlike womenswear and menswear, childrenswear often looks to the European luxury market to discover the latest in kids' fashion.

To predict market changes, visit retail stores as a means of understanding what your competitors are offering, what is and isn't selling well, and even what is being shown in the teen and young adult market. As children want to look like an older brother and sister, trends from the 7–14 and 8–20 size categories often trickle down into childrenswear with modified proportions, colors, and details. However, how quickly and literally these trends filter down into your brand will be determined by your customer's willingness to change and try new ideas. So, when devising your portfolio, create some groups that reflect current influences from the older market and some that cater to a younger, more traditional customer.

Thematic inspirations

Whereas the womenswear market utilizes highly sophisticated inspirations from which a designer will research and develop a collection in terms of detail, motif, and garment concept, childrenswear collections often rely on more obvious and less cerebral themes. From such pop-culture influences as comic strips and celebrities to whimsical aspects of ethnic and historical costume, designers are given full creative license to develop work that is both playful and highly coordinated.

Childrenswear specialty areas

Infants
Baby layettes that include wrapped garments, rompers or "onesies," diaper pants, dresses, seasonal outerwear, Henley T-shirts, sweater knits, and cotton knits.

Toddler boys and girls
Ensembles and separates, rompers, overalls, shirts.

Sportswear
Coats, jackets, shirts, tailored looks, denim, sweater knits, T-shirts, swimsuits, jumpers.

Dresses
Party dresses, ensembles, jumpers with blouses, casual daytime dresses.

Sleepwear and lingerie
Nightgowns, pajamas, slips, nightshirts, robes, hosiery, undergarments.

Outerwear
Formal and casual coats, casual jackets, winter parkas, snowsuits, rainwear.

◀ MINI ME
For some brands, childrenswear receives fashion direction from the teens market. Silhouettes, colors, graphics, and even accessories reflect a consumer who aspires to look like his or her older brother or sister! However, interpretations must always be age-appropriate.

Build a winning childrenswear portfolio

Although there are elements of a childrenswear portfolio that apply to all categories and markets, there are specific requirements within this category. These range from how you present the work so that it speaks to the age group, the types of inspiration you use to generate interest and sales, and the design parameters demanded by parents. Bear in mind the following when putting together a childrenswear portfolio:

1 Layout
A horizontal format best communicates the age and attitude of the category. As with page composition, the scale of the figure and the size of the book should always be considered in order to underscore the intended message.

2 Research foundations
When devising the portfolio groups, ensure that your themes and inspirations are whimsical, happy, fun, and child-friendly. Common themes include historical costume, ethnic inspirations, children's literature, and pop-culture references such as cartoon and movie characters. These themes allow design to be highly contextural and detailed, while maintaining a close relationship with the original source. Whereas fashion designers for adult clothing may utilize a theme for translating into deeper meanings, childrenswear concepts should be immediate and approachable.

3 Presentation
The croquis book and portfolio will be required components during the interview process. Because the childrenswear industry designs largely through garment flats, be

▼ OPPOSITE PERSONALITIES
The femininity of Claude Monet's artwork and the modern neon sculptures of Bruce Nauman give this collection a unique contrast. Feminine ruffles and pastel colors in cotton evolve into neon colors and synthetic, shiny fabrics.

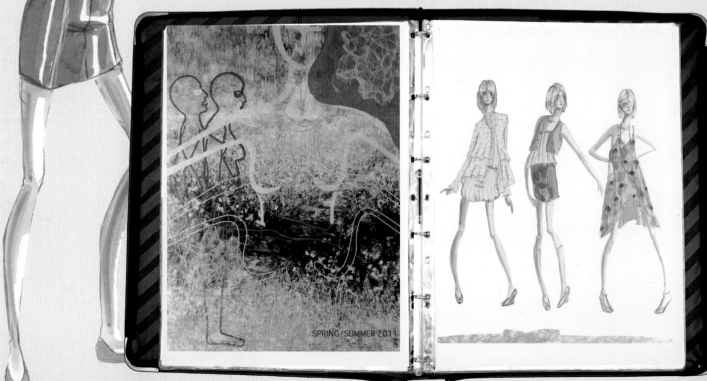

SPRING/SUMMER 2011

aware of how you convey your design process. Figures will add visual interest and attitude to the portfolio and croquis book, but the increase of flats in your sketchbook will showcase not only design detail and specificity, but also your ability to transition from the classroom to the professional design room.

4 Classifications

Within your graduate portfolio, it is advisable to showcase a range of age groups. Although you will probably specialize in a particular age and gender as your career develops, a breadth of work not only will reveal your creative range and versatility, but also will demonstrate your desirability as an employee, no matter which brand you interview with. In addition to age, display a range of themes, color stories, and fabrications that are suitable for specific areas of childrenswear, such as denimwear and party dresses. Portfolios typically showcase either boyswear or girlswear, although a mixture may be shown.

▲▶ KALEIDOSCOPIC COLOR CLASH
Childrenswear colors and patterns are rarely somber and serious. Cheerful, bright, and saturated colors used in contrasting combinations accentuate a highly energized and playful attitude.

Common childrenswear fabrications

- Auto-repeat stripes
- Printed knits
- Novelty yarns and sweater knits
- Cotton eyelet
- Yarn-dyed woven stripes
- Small-scale floral prints
- Novelty prints (also called conversational prints, e.g., automobiles, cartoon characters)
- Embroideries
- Denim and chambray
- Cotton twills
- Terry, fleece, and other dense textures
- Yarn-dyed gingham, madras, and plaids
- Silk-screen prints and graphics

Childrenswear IS...	Childrenswear ISN'T...
WASHABLE	DRY-CLEAN FABRICS
INEXPENSIVE FABRICS	TAILORED
DENIMS AND TWILLS	FORMAL
KNITWEAR	UNCOMFORTABLE FIT OR FABRICS
TEXTURED	DIFFICULT TO PUT ON OR TAKE OFF
COTTONS	MINIMALISM
FABRIC TREATMENTS	TONAL COLORS
SATURATED COLORS AND PASTELS	BLACK
CHILD-SAFE	LARGE-SCALE PRINTS
POP-CULTURE	DULL COLOR STORIES
THEMATIC	SERIOUS OR CEREBRAL
WHIMSICAL AND FANTASTICAL	SCULPTURAL SILHOUETTE
PRINTS	CONCEPTUAL
LIGHT HEARTED	MOODY
PLAYFUL	AVANT-GARDE

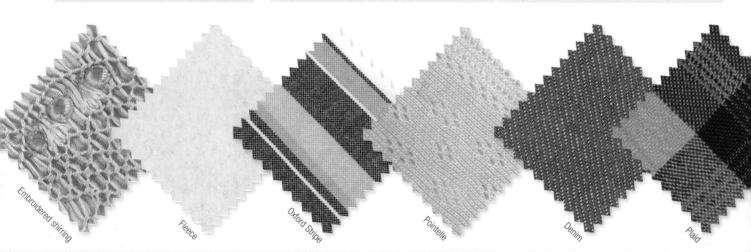

Embroidered shirring   Fleece   Oxford Stripe   Pointelle   Denim   Plaid

Checklist: Build a winning childrenswear portfolio

- Have you shown awareness of a child's developmental stages and physical abilities?
- Are the collections highly thematic to create whimsy and fantasy?

- Are the silhouettes familiar? Do all of the design details happen within the prescribed silhouette?
- Are the collections for the younger market highly coordinated and offered in multiple colorways?

- Do the fabrications largely consist of washable cottons?
- Have you ensured that color reigns supreme and avoided black to reflect a typical parent's preferences?

- Have you defined your groups by using different poses and attitudes to help identify the child's age?

KIDS WITH A CAUSE

Kidswear often reflects a parent's aesthetic and, in some cases, global concerns. The increase of global awareness, sustainability, and eco-friendly fabrics seen in the adult market is also very much present in the childrenswear market.

Targeting your portfolio:
Teenager wear/Juniors

A portfolio for the teenage category offers the designer an ideal opportunity to portray large quantities of trend-oriented designs with great creative freedom.

As consumers with newly found spending power, teenagers are eager to view the latest offerings from the fashion design world. They represent a unique market because, for the first time in their lives, they are no longer subject to their parents' fashion choices and are the decisionmakers when choosing what to buy. Teenagers' exposure to pop culture and the influence of their peers greatly inform their aesthetic choices. Fashion that is deemed "in" by their peer group may suddenly become old news within days. A teenager's desire to be accepted by a particular group and to use fashion as a visual symbol for tribal allegiance is profoundly important. This finicky attitude toward fashion, as well as the desire for the latest "in-fashion" item, makes the junior market a rapidly changing one.

In the middle

The positioning of the junior market and its associated aesthetic bridges the unique characteristics of both the children's and adults' markets. Young teenagers retain much of their visual aesthetics from childhood, such as bright colors and pronounced visual textures, yet wish to gain a level of independence from their parents. As they start to discover the world, they gravitate toward clothing that draws on the sensibilities of childrenswear, but that is cut in adult silhouettes. Girls wish to look like their cool older sister, whereas boys often gravitate toward men's clothing that is cut to their size. For each gender, the community's culture and the influence of peers often play an integral role in shaping teenage fashion choices, because most wish to be accepted by the community above all else.

◀▲ **BETWEEN STAGES**
The juniors market displays characteristics that are often colorful like childrenswear, yet grown up in silhouette. When developing your portfolio, washable and affordable fabrics will ensure that your collections stay category specific.

Checklist: Build a winning teenager wear portfolio

- Have you shown that you understand the impact of a teenager's consumer power?
- Does your portfolio reflect a teenage love of bright colors and strong textures?

- Have you considered the importance of teenage social groupings?
- Do you show evidence of being able to adapt to the changing demands of the junior market?

- Does your portfolio successfully straddle the junior and adult markets?
- Have you paid close attention to sizing?

- Are the fabrics swatches in your collection inexpensive?
- Do you show a good understanding of a teenager's search for identity through clothing?

Specific design considerations

Whereas some elements of design may trickle down from the adult world, the speed with which each trend is adopted and discarded demands that designers maintain a closer connection to the customer's pop culture than any other market. When designing for the teenage market, consider the following market characteristics:

The new fit

The junior girl's body is developing into adult shapes and proportions. As such, curvaceous hips, a defined waist, and rounded breasts all begin to play a role in design and production considerations. Sizes are 3, 5, 7, 9, 11, and 13 and begin to mirror adult garment patterns through body contouring and fit, although overall garment scale tends to be smaller.

Fast fashion

As a population with newly discovered consumer power, the typical junior customer often uses shopping as a form of social recreation with friends. This coupling of consumerism with entertainment, as well as a body that is still growing and frequently in need of new clothes, creates a market that demands new products faster than designer price-point collections. As a result of this "fast fashion" and teenage budget, fabrics are often inexpensive and garment longevity is of low priority. The consumers' ever-shifting tastes and desire for what is fashionable call for a never-ending supply of new products in the stores.

Shopping for an identity

Most consumers, regardless of age, view their fashion choices as hallmarks of who they are. Such choices also serve as signs of aspiration, and this is no truer than in the junior market. Are they part of the preppy cheerleader group or the out-of-fashion nerds? Do they wear clothing that signifies their desire to be a nonconformist through the adoption of the punk uniform or do they prefer to blend in with the community by adopting a more generic wardrobe? You only have to watch the movie *The Breakfast Club* (1985) to understand the tribes that teenagers create within the broader social network. As social media expands and the consumer's desire for a unique identity increases, the complexities of group demographics will increase and force designers to be more highly attuned to their customers' needs.

▶ **TOMORROW'S WOMAN**
Sophisticated colors, textures, and proportions give this collection a confident, grown-up attitude. Because the junior market is often inspired by trends that percolate the adult markets, consider how these can be adjusted for a more youthful audience.

Targeting your portfolio:
Activewear

- THE IMPORTANCE OF TECHNOLOGICAL ADVANCES
- HOW TO PUT TOGETHER AN ACTIVEWEAR PORTFOLIO

Activewear portfolios evolve continuously due to newly discovered technologies, shifting fashion trends, and competitive athletes' demands. From the mass-market brands of Nike and Adidas to designers such as Stella McCartney and Yohji Yamamoto, activewear is available at every price point.

Before such luminaries as Gabrielle "Coco" Chanel (1883–1971), clothing worn for leisurely activities like tennis, swimming, and hunting were designed according to the daywear silhouettes and fabrications of the period. Modesty and an adherence to social mandates were the priority rather than performance. For example, swimming at seaside resorts involved wearing heavy black or navy wool suits and stockings that concealed the body, and offered minimal respite from the heat and unsuccessful buoyancy in the water.

When sporting activities finally became fashionable for the middle classes during the 1920s (and women gained greater independence from strict social mores), designers began to address the concept of sportswear that enabled women to change clothes for specific activities. A key factor in the development of today's activewear was Chanel's use of jersey fabric, which had previously been relegated to men's undergarments; the knitted fabric allowed for increased movement and breathability during strenuous activity. The history of sports clothing continued with tennis player René Lacoste fashioning the polo top in the 1920s, DuPont inventing nylon in 1935 and spandex in 1959, and Patagonia leading the eco-friendly movement of using fabrics made from organic cottons and fleece (developed in 1993 from discarded plastic soda bottles).

A changing role

Today's advances in fabric and design technology have resulted in fabrics that provide protection from the sun, welded seams for waterproofing, odor-controlling fibers, fabrics that change color because of increases in body temperature, and even graphic

◀ A BYGONE ERA
Unlike these wool suits from the turn of the twentieth century, today's activewear is about maximizing performance. Cumbersome bathing costumes have given way to production and fabric technology that is transforming competitive sports and Olympic records.

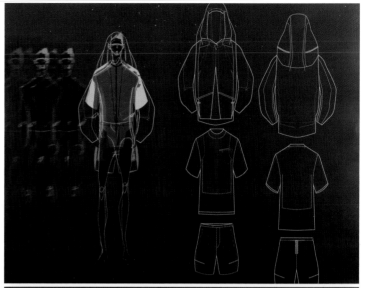

◀▲ AQUATIC TECHNOLOGY
Speedo's LZR Racer was designed by using computer software with tremendous success. Of the 37 world records gained in the 2010 Olympics, swimmers wore the suit for 35 of them.

designs that are revealed when the garment is photographed through a process called kameraflage. Fabric technology, like computer technology, is evolving daily, and how this will affect design and athletic performance remains to be seen.

Activewear is a multibillion dollar, global business that has transformed the clothing once only worn for playing sports into fashionable daywear. Given the popularity of wearing athletic clothing that reveals team support, sporting fashion can carry great cultural meaning and indicate to which tribe one belongs. Although the key characteristics of activewear will remain comfort and performance, the colors and insignia of the team you choose to wear can promote fraternity or friendly discord depending on the environment in which the garment is worn!

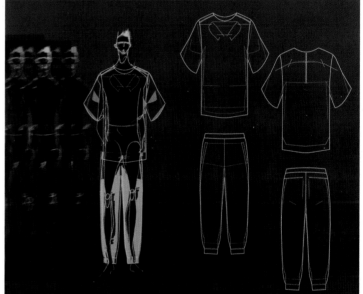

▲ PRESENTATION AS A SUGGESTION OF PRODUCT
The new advances in activewear technology are suggested in this layout design. By using such art direction in your portfolio, you are able to underscore the collection's mood while flaunting your skills.

Checklist: Build a winning activewear portfolio

- Have you taken into account how advances in fabric technology affect activewear design?

- Do you show an understanding of the importance of activewear to the consumer for declaring team allegiance?

- Have you considered the comfort levels of your garment designs?

- Does your portfolio show your activewear designs to be specific to a sport or activity?

- Do your designs successfully combine technological advances with smart design?

- Have you used colors and color placements to enhance the collection?

- Have you experienced the activity firsthand for which you are designing garments?

- Have you assessed within your portfolio the look and feel of the activewear, as well as how it will be used?

6 hallmarks of successful activewear

Certain characteristics contribute to this category's appeal and identity. Consider the following attributes when creating your collections and portfolio.

1 Comfort

As one of the defining characteristics of activewear, comfort is critical for commercial success. Whether your collections are for use on the soccer field or the chic après-ski lounge, customers demand clothing that is unlike their typical daytime wardrobe. Consider the choice of fabrications, garment fit, areas that require stretch and movement, and where the body generates the most heat. If your designs feel in the least bit awkward or do not allow for maximum movement, the consumer will shop elsewhere.

2 Performance

Garments must serve the requirements of specific sporting activities. Traditionally, designs suited a range of different sports. Today's brands realize that research—and smart marketing—create dynamic products that reflect the intricacies of each sport. Designers interview athletes, analyze their movements, and consider fabrics and construction that will enhance performance. Far from being solely a fashion designer, the activewear designer must be attuned to physiology, ergonomics, and the sport itself.

3 Fabrication and smart design

The chemistry involved in developing fabrics that can draw moisture away from the body and provide maximum breathability, as well as materials that actually improve performance are revolutionizing the athletic world. As an activewear designer, your ability to bridge the most recent fabric technologies with smart design is critical for the market's future and your own relevance as a designer. Aside from

▶ ENERGIZING GRAPHICS

Bold, jarring asymmetrical graphics give a sense of energy and motion to designs. When developing your activewear, incorporate bold color contrasts to move the eye, and highlight areas of the body.

▼ AESTHETIC PERFORMANCE

Today's sports enthusiasts demand products that surpass performance and meet their aesthetic impulses. A surge of new brands cater to these diverse aesthetics and range from Chanel to The North Face.

developments in fabrication, the innovations in garment manufacturing must also be researched. From customized bodysuits utilizing the 3-D body scanner to welded seams that minimize overall garment weight, advances in both the lab and the factory serve to improve athletic performance.

4 Color

How do you feel when you view a tonal color story? Does your impression change when viewing vibrant, graphic color relationships? Activewear designers are highly attuned to the emotional impact of color when creating color palettes and placements in each design and collection. Sports clothing typically uses graphic color relationships, which make the garments and wearer appear active, unlike tonal colors that can suggest the wearer is relaxed. Many designs use graphic shapes to highlight specific areas of the anatomy that are frequently used in a particular sport.

▶ OLYMPIC DISCO
This sequined swimsuit gives evidence to the high aesthetic demands consumers have placed on activewear. Although functionality underscores the market's products, designers must create collections that are fashion-forward.

5 Experimental designing

Given the specificity of garment usage, it's not surprising that many designers practice the sport for which they are designing. By experiencing the sport, wearer's demands, existing silhouettes and fabrications, and how wear-and-tear occurs, the designer becomes an informed researcher for the next collection. Performing the activity also provides design ideas for what is needed both pre- and post-sporting activity, along with accessories to improve the user's experience. Gaining an understanding of how your consumer utilizes and experiences activewear will provide you with the tools for future innovation in a rapidly evolving market.

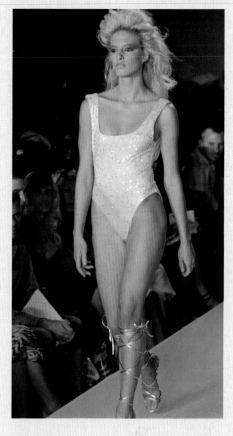

6 Usage

It is estimated that 75 percent of all swimwear never touches water, which indicates that many consumers buy activewear for how it looks and feels rather than for performance reasons. As fashion designers, the opportunity to create athletic clothing in which design and aesthetic are in such high demand is exciting. When designing your collections, target your fashion based on how your consumer will use the garments. Would she be interested in a suede bikini with decorative, jewelry-like details or require a wetsuit that uses the latest advances in fabric technology to give her added edge during competitions?

◀ THE URBAN SLOPES
Athletes often bridge their sporting activities with their daily routine by appropriating activewear for every occasion. Consider how your collections could transition between sport-specific activities and the urban landscape.

Knitwear

- **THE KEY CRITERIA FOR KNITWEAR DESIGN**
- **WHAT MAKES A STRONG KNITWEAR PORTFOLIO**

As an element of nearly every portfolio and collection, knitwear is offered at every price point, design category, aesthetic, customer type, and season.

Knitwear is essential for creating a well-merchandised collection. Depending upon the knit structure and fiber, it can be draped like chiffon or tailored like wool gabardine, and it can even serve as outerwear. From the gauge sizes of yarn, fibers available, stitches possible, and techniques applied, knitwear is considered by many to be fashion design at its most conceptual and inventive.

Because of the complexity of creating the fabric and form from scratch, designers who have technical proficiency coupled with design talent are in high demand. Your portfolio must always flaunt your knowledge and talent, and the knitwear category is an excellent area in which to do so.

Knitwear: A diverse category

When structuring your portfolio groups, it is helpful to utilize knitwear for its unique characteristics and ease of wear. From forms that require minimal construction for slim fit to architectural silhouettes that may be more comfortable than their woven imitations, knitwear is often seen as an addition to a designer's collection, particularly when diversifying motif and color relationships. Knitwear may even be the signature and focus of the brand, as seen at houses such as TSE and Missoni.

▼▶ KNITTED SOFTWARE
Computer-aided design (CAD) is used by many designers to create and technically perfect their ideas. Technology makes the complex stitches and color transition of this design a possibility for mainstream production.

KNIT DEVELOPMENT

Key knitwear features

When designing knitwear for your portfolio, keep the following points in mind:

1 Samples make it real
Always show the actual knitted swatch to explain your consideration of gauge, yarn, and stitch, rather than a yarn reeling.

2 Needles and machines
To flaunt your proficiency, show both hand-knitted swatches and machine-knitted designs. Having experience across the many methods of producing knitwear conveys not only a good level of experience, but also your interest and passion for the medium.

3 The auxiliary portfolio
If you have a relatively high level of experience with developing knitted swatches and wish to make a solid commitment to pursuing knitwear, an additional book containing swatch development is a great idea when interviewing. Whereas your portfolio will showcase how you conceive collections, your swatch book will demonstrate creative and technical acumen.

4 Exploring all areas
Knitwear isn't just relegated to heavy wool sweaters! Remember to explore every conceivable category, weight, application, choice of material, and level of detail. The possibilities for knitwear are limitless and include cashmere evening knits encrusted with beading or embroidery, high-performance tech-fabrics that respond to body temperature by changing color, and accessories that are made from knitted suede cord.

▲ UNEXPECTED POSSIBILITIES
The diversity for knitwear development is endless, as shown in this light-weight, transparent knitted dress. By exploring the versatility of the fabric, your breadth of category and item will be expanded exponentially.

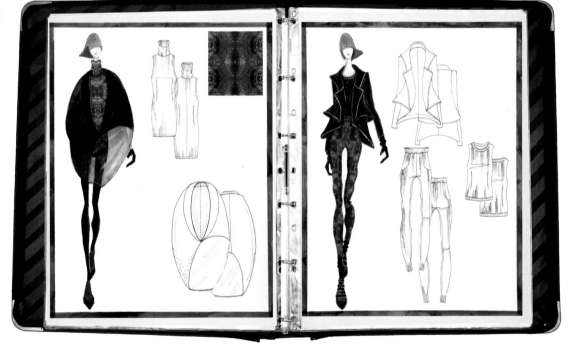

Checklist: Build a winning knitwear portfolio

- Have you shown full exploration of the design versatility of knitwear?
- Have you improved your technical (as well as your design) knowledge of knitwear?

(Turn to pages 154–155 for useful knitwear terminology that can be incorporated into your portfolio pages.)
- Do you have both hand-knitted and machine-knitted swatches of your knitwear designs in your portfolio?
- Do you have an auxiliary portfolio containing swatch examples?

- Have you analyzed all the different weights and categories of knitwear?
- Have you explored knitted accessories as well as garments?

Targeting your portfolio:
Bridal wear

• THE SPECIAL REQUIREMENTS OF BRIDAL WEAR DESIGN
• PRODUCE A STUNNING BRIDAL WEAR PORTFOLIO

Designing a dress for a wedding, one of the most important events in a woman's life, is often an intimate and creative experience. Increasingly, brides are looking for something unique, and your portfolio must show awareness of her demands.

▶ CELEBRATING INDIVIDUALITY
Today's bride demands a more personalized expression when creating her special day. The portfolio must reflect diverse aesthetics and ceremony contexts through fabrication, treatments, lengths, dresses, and separates.

As an area of design that will always be in demand, the bridal sector is global, ageless, and relevant to all cultures. The bride's dress and the other garments associated with a wedding party are designed purely for fantasy and the "wow" factor. Bridal dresses are worn only for a few hours, yet they become indelible memories as photographs and videos are viewed for decades to come. As such, the choice of fabric, silhouette, embellishment, and overall aesthetic carries great weight for the customer.

Unlike the development of traditional sportswear portfolios, where the concept of mix-and-match is essential for offering one-stop shopping, bridal dresses are singular purchases and are created by a designer who gains a reputation for his or her general aesthetic. Whether they are offered by designers such as Vera Wang, whose bridal gowns are world renowned and offer a multitude of shapes and approaches, or houses such as Chanel couture that feature a bride at the end of every show, the future bride decides whose work to consider based upon the house's targeted customer and price point. It's worth noting that the need for affordable bridal dresses is so high that retailers such as J. Crew and Ann Taylor have entered this category with great success. There are even some designers who may not offer a bridal line per se, but will cut their existing evening wear in white fabrics so that customers have a bridal option.

◀ COUTURE DETAILS
A dress of such importance deserves to be of the highest quality. Bridal designers have a high understanding of garment construction in order to create made-to-measure dresses that are often passed down for generations.

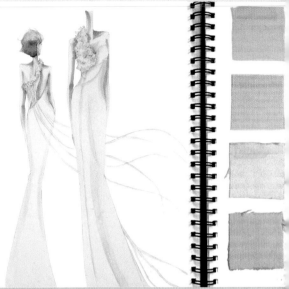

▼ RELAXED ROMANTICISM
The gap between the bridal category and current fashion trends is growing narrower as consumers desire gowns that reflect their sophisticated and personalized tastes. The clean lines, lack of glitz, and simple sheath construction of this bridal gown conveys a relaxed yet romantic attitude to suit a modern customer.

Key hallmarks of the bridal market

Keep in mind the following criteria when designing for the bridal market:

Creativity and fantasy trumps all

Because of the cultural symbolism placed on a wedding dress and the short period of time for which it will be worn, creativity—rather than practicality—is of paramount importance. Most brides want a magical and memorable day, and wearing a special dress that transports them from the everyday is part of the ritual. You will need to consider silhouette, embellishments, fabric choices, and even comfort.

Know the internal workings

Traditional bridal gowns and their more modern equivalents can have a large amount of understructure. Like couture, understanding how these components work to create design is essential for achieving the gown's desired silhouette and fit. This technical proficiency plays an integral role during the rigorous fitting sessions, in which a sophisticated understanding of construction is needed. As a student, you must learn these construction techniques in order to support your design.

Step outside tradition

Not every woman wants the iconic, yet traditional, full-scale bridal dress in white silk satin. Because most bridal designers show portfolios that are a mixture of bridal and evening wear, consider how evening wear silhouettes and fabrics could be adapted for the bridal market. Narciso Rodriguez revolutionized how we perceive bridal wear when he designed a minimal white sheath for Carolyn Bessette's wedding to John F. Kennedy, Jr. Similarly, John Galliano's blush-stained hem on Gwen Stefani's wedding dress reminded us that color is highly effective in the wedding dress context.

Second time around

As a part of today's culture, many women will have more than one wedding during their lifetime. For such occasions, the desire for an understated ceremony may require a dress that is less ornate than that worn at the first wedding, or perhaps even a tailored wedding suit. Adding this market demographic to your bridal portfolio shows that you are not only attuned to the market's needs, but are also able to design for a variety of ages and aesthetics. When designing for the older customer, comfort—rather than dramatic silhouettes and corsets—is often a priority, along with mature colors, fabrics, and less revealing silhouettes.

Close relationships

Depending upon the nature of your design room, it may be standard practice to work closely with the client when selecting her dress and to allow for design modifications based on her requests. Like the couture sector, changes in detail, beading layout, fabrications, and even silhouette may be required. Once the selections have been made and a muslin, or toile, has been sewn, repeated fittings are performed. It can be either enjoyable or challenging to work with a customer on such an important event, but the high level of creativity can make it rewarding.

The full party

As a bridal designer, you are expected to provide dresses for the remainder of the bridal party. These may include the bridesmaid dresses, the flower girl's dress, and the mother of the bride's outfit. Although these designs may be less involved, the aesthetic must adhere to the bride's requests. It is common to perform multiple fittings on each member of the party.

◀ **FULL SUITE AHEAD**
Bridal designers must consider all aspects of dressing the bridal party such as the bridesmaids. By using your knowledge for developing collections, you will be able to create a cohesive grouping that still allows the bride to shine.

▶ FITTING MAKES PERFECT

It is not uncommon for top bridal houses to perform multiple fittings on the bride-to-be. Once the dress is selected, fittings are scheduled during the weeks leading up to the event in an effort to perfect this important milestone.

Endless opportunities

Working within the bridal industry will enable you to work wherever you wish. Unlike most major fashion houses based in the fashion capitals of New York, Paris, and Milan, bridal designers can create their own studios wherever there is an audience. Additionally, unlike sportswear, the narrower range of fabrics allows designers to order yardage that can be kept for years to come without having to adhere to trends or choreographing complex color and fabric palettes!

▼ IT'S ALL RELATIVE

Bridal portfolios frequently include cocktail and evening collections due to their similarities. It is not uncommon for evening wear designers to recut silhouettes in white to target the bridal sector, and vice versa!

Checklist: Build a winning bridal wear portfolio

- Have you considered all aspects of bridal dress design, including fabric, silhouette, and decorative detailing?

- Is creativity your driving force rather than practicality?

- Have you shown a full understanding of the complex structuring and construction techniques of a bridal gown?

- Can you adapt any of your evening wear items for bridal wear?

- Do your designs take into account the tastes and needs of those marrying for a second time?

- Have you stated in your portfolio whether you would be prepared to work closely with the bride to create a perfect gown?

- Are you prepared to create items for the extended bridal party such as bridesmaids? If so, show evidence of this in your portfolio.

Targeting your portfolio:
Accessories

- **THE KEY SKILLS OF AN ACCESSORY DESIGNER**
- **HOW TO CREATE AN ACCESSORY PORTFOLIO**

As one of the largest-growing areas in the fashion industry, accessories have gained unprecedented attention from both designers and consumers. As a designer, your portfolio should cover a breadth of item and product use, along with evidence of technical acumen.

Accessory design: Skills and requirements

An aspiring fashion accessory designer is typically exposed to the following areas of design:

- Old and current fashion trends
- Fashion history survey
- Accessory design survey
- Conceptual development
- Digital skills such as Photoshop and Illustrator
- Fashion drawing and design
- Textile and surface design
- Fashion marketing and advertising
- Prototype development
- Construction techniques
- Materiality

Virtually every fashion house today offers accessories to complete the brand's creative portfolio and fulfill their customer's needs. Developing an accessories portfolio is not unlike creating the more standard fashion design book. Groups will be arranged according to particular inspirations with corresponding color palettes and fabrications, and such categories as career, weekend, evening, and even athletic may inspire certain items, fabrications, and silhouettes that all target one defined customer. Although the addressing of seasons may appear less obvious than clothing, collections are typically designed with a season in mind, particularly if they are to complement the new trends.

Accessory design is highly sculptural and ergonomic in nature, and it requires an expert in 3-D form. Items may range from a wide category of shoes, millinery, bags, and small leather goods. The accessory design portfolio may also be supported by textile designs, computer specs to demonstrate technical knowledge, designs for hardware or wax castings, and images of samples made to illustrate manufacturing experience. Regardless of the

▼ THE URBAN RANCH
Forming rich, contextual themes is just as critical for accessory designers as for their clothing counterparts. By composing color and textile palettes that denote a particular theme and lifestyle, your collections remain cohesive and unique. Always consider how your brand separates you from today's competition.

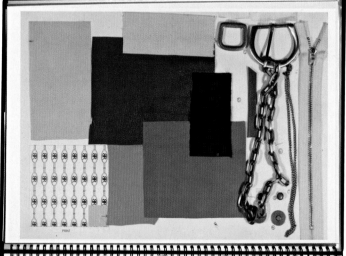

Checklist: Build a winning accessories portfolio

- Are you sufficiently demonstrating your versatility across the accessory spectrum?
- Do you show a good understanding of three-dimensional design?

- Does your portfolio display appropriate computer skills in Photoshop and Illustrator?
- Do you show a wide knowledge and understanding of the accessories market?

- Can you adapt your designs to different price points?
- Have you proven your awareness of trends in the accessory market?
- Do you show exceptional creative and innovative skills?

- Have you adequately explored different accessory materials?
- Do your designs reflect both the decorative and the practical uses of accessories?

portfolio's inner structure, maintaining a focused customer alongside a diversity of product is key. Although you may wish to be a shoe designer at a high-end label, flaunting your creativity and aesthetic through a diversity of product design will only serve to indicate how marketable you are.

The dynamic portfolio

A critical point to remember when designing accessories is to use a wide spectrum of fabrications, hardware, and silhouettes. Within these, you must be very specific, right down to the hardware design and type of finish you want for the metal components. Also, it is essential to research materials beyond leather! Consider how such unconventional materials and treatments as wood, plastic, beading, embroidery, denim, and even knitwear could be made into accessories. You only have to look at the broad offering of athletic footwear on offer to realize that nearly any material (and type of technology) can be incorporated into accessory design. When you consider the future of accessory design and consumer needs, how will these shape your portfolio groupings?

Always approach accessories as forms of sculpture that can be used for purely decorative reasons (e.g., jewelry), for utilitarian reasons (e.g., backpacks), or to serve both purposes, as seen with many high-end footwear brands. A portfolio that showcases the many diverse ways in which accessories may be used demonstrates both the designer's talent and relevance in today's market.

Key attributes of a successful accessory designer

Although accessory designers and fashion designers have certain attributes in common, there are key characteristics that are crucial for a successful accessory designer.

- A sharp eye for detail design and engineering
- Strong comprehension of 3-D design
- Ability to evaluate ergonomics and a product's usage
- Strong skills in CAD (computer-aided design)
- Understanding of marketing and sales principles
- Strong interpersonal and leadership skills when working with a design team
- Ability to analyze and target a customer demographic and a consumer's particular needs
- Broad knowledge of the accessory market and accessory trends
- Exceptional creativity and innovation
- Understanding of accessory manufacturing and global industry
- Ability to adapt design for various price points
- High level of visual and verbal articulation of design concepts

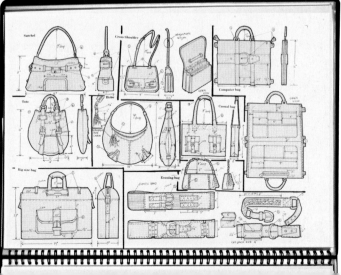

Going professional

The transition from a nurturing school environment that allows a degree of freedom to the professional arena, where you must perform for an employer, can be jarring. However, strategic planning and work experience can make the transition both seamless and rewarding.

Perhaps one of the most important benchmarks in your life is the day you become a young professional. This is the moment that your acquired knowledge and expertise is put to use in the real world. In order to make this transition a successful one, you must research the job market, have a deep understanding of yourself, and enter the practice confidently. For many graduates, summer jobs during high school and college provide insights into professionalism, responsibility, and how to be a team player. Added to these are internships that will give you direct experience in fashion design, hopefully across several company cultures.

Although you may be intent on being a fashion designer, the varieties of corporate cultures that exist are as diverse as the collections themselves. By experiencing a variety of design rooms, you will be able to select the type that most allows you to succeed when entering the professional world.

Internships and interviews:
Getting started

- **WRITE A RÉSUMÉ AND COVER LETTER**
- **DEVELOP AN EMPLOYER LIST**

Fashion is a highly competitive industry and landing an internship or your first job takes time, effort, and patience.

Ideally, you should work at least one internship during your undergraduate education. It can be for one summer or last for several school semesters. Many resources exist for finding internship opportunities, including:

- The career center at your school
- Your professors
- Online fashion industry and corporate websites
- Classmates, colleagues, family, and friends

Teal blue double face silk charmeuse top with large front pleat.

Black Kangaroo leather cigarette pant.

Charcoal gray cashmere double layer curved coat with gray silk charmeuse lining.

Gray hand knit lamb wool and mohair mixed oversize bobble sweater.

Charcoal gray laquered wool wide square leg pants with sculpted pocketrs.

Black lamb leather cropped jacket with over the shoulder curved panels and quilted collar and side panels.

Light gray lamb leather hooded vest with curved front opening lined in light gray merino wool.

Dark gray wool jersey top with curved seaming and pleat details on side hem and sleeves.

Black double layer silk gazar skirt with volumized pleat details on hem lined in sateen silk organza.

Light gray laquered wool day-dress with raglan sleeve and curved panels.

Blue Iris mink vest with mixed sheared and long hair curved pieces.

Matt silver sequins race-back tank with circle metal buttons on center back opening.

Light gray laquered wool cropped pant with curved hem and curved sculpted pockets.

Black and white textured wool-cashmere coat with black lamb leather panel in front and back and one-piece sleeve.

Black and teal blue double face silk charmeuse dress with curved continious seamings form front to back and oversize over the shoulder silk sateen collar.

Silver sequins and silk brocade mixed panel fitted dress and open back detail.

Blue Iris mink coat with mixed sheared and long hair curved pieces lined in matt silver silk charmeuse.

Employer list

Identify and categorize your ideal employers before you start job-hunting to save time and help you strategize your approach. Most likely, they will all share a similar aesthetic and customer base. A list can also help you focus on choosing the best job for your future career rather than the first job that comes along. Some key questions to consider are:

1 What are the top three goals for your career? (e.g., Starting your own line in five years, working for a prestigious European designer.)

2 Who are your top seven favorite designers? What is it that you like most and least about each of them?

3 How do your likes and dislikes align with your top three career goals?

4 Categorize each designer from one to seven. Your one to seven listing will be your "best employers" list. It will be your ideal/top list of employers. Then, identify two more sets of potential employers. These will be your "better employers" and "good employers" lists. To do so, go through steps 2 to 4 once more. These will be your secondary and tertiary lists of prospective employers. As you go through the following stages, refer back to these lists and make sure you pursue opportunities at these employers first and foremost.

◄ **THE LINE SHEET**
A professionally produced line sheet with your résumé printed on the reverse side provides an impressive view of your abilities to your interviewer. Line sheets may show the entire thesis collection or selected images of your work and aesthetic.

The types of internships available vary greatly. For larger companies such as Banana Republic or Tommy Hilfiger, you might intern within a specific area such as Women's Sweater Knits or Men's Wovens. Smaller houses, such as Thakoon or Chris Benz, may expose you to the entire spectrum of the collection, while also allowing you to perform such hands-on tasks as pattern making or draping, and virtually anything else that needs to get done!

It is important that you experience various types of internships while you are a student, so that you can learn what type of design room culture you are best suited to.

Writing a résumé

Hundreds of books have been written about how to write a fantastic résumé. These can be very helpful in providing examples of the multiple formats for résumés. However, keep in mind that the best résumé that exists is the one that secures an interview. If you haven't had a formal job before, you may think you have little to include on a résumé. However, résumés are also strong tools for promoting your academic successes and unique skills. Is your GPA 3.5? That might be something you want an employer to know. Are you an accomplished freelance tailor? That demonstrates a commitment to fashion and a working knowledge of garment construction.

Write your résumé in the format that highlights your strongest points, whether they are academic-, employment-, or skills-oriented. When it's complete and nearly perfect, ask someone who has knowledge of résumés to review and edit it for you. If you don't know anyone with this skill, there are a multitude of resources online that will review and edit your résumé for a fee.

Talk to everyone you know

Job leads can come from anywhere, and the best way to find out about as many of these as possible is to mention your job search to everyone you know, including family, friends, classmates, professors, and acquaintances. Tell them exactly what you want to do and find out if they know anyone in the industry. If they do, ask them if they'd feel comfortable giving you a referral. If they say "no," thank them politely and move on to the next subject.

However, if they do offer to help, thank them and ask what they need from you to make this important connection. They may say, "Send me a copy of your résumé, and I'll send it on to [Mike Smith]." In this case, write a cover letter addressed directly to Mike Smith. Email your contact both the résumé and cover letter, and ask him or her to please forward both to Mr. Smith. And remember to thank your contact for his or her help.

Checklist: Getting an interview

- Have you worked at least one internship as an undergraduate?
- Have your internships helped you identify the type of design room in which you will thrive professionally?

- Have you identified your top three career goals?
- Have you selected your top seven fashion designers?
- Have you listed your three groups of potential employers?

- Does your résumé include all your key skills and achievements?
- Have you structured your cover letter correctly and identified the right recipient?

- Have you used word-of-mouth to secure an interview?
- Are you being sufficiently proactive and persistent in your search?

Writing a cover letter

Although your résumé lists your accomplishments and skills and should, therefore, be all a recruiter needs from you, a cover letter is mandatory for any job application. There are two key points to bear in mind when writing and editing a cover letter:

- The reader's attention span
- The job description's key words

Employers will typically spend between thirty seconds and three minutes reading your résumé and cover letter. This is your reader's attention span, and how much time he or she spends on your application is almost entirely dependent upon the total number of other applications he or she needs to review. Your cover letter is your one opportunity to make the reader want to call you in for an interview. Key rules of thumb for writing your cover letter include:

1 Keep it succinct
Use two to three sentences per paragraph and a maximum of five paragraphs for the entire letter. Also, remember that bulleted lists can convey a lot of information in a small amount of space.

2 Use the key words included in the job description
If the job description says "strong skills in construction and illustration," for example, then make sure you use these exact words in your cover letter, and provide information about where or how you acquired that skill.

3 Always use a name
Never send an application to the HR Department or "To Whom It May Concern." A search on the Internet should enable you to find the key personnel at the company to which you're applying, whether it's the Director of HR or the VP of Design. Always address your letter to this person. Whatever you do, never send out any résumé (or cover letter) without having someone else proofread it first!

If your contact offers to help in a more general way, such as "I'll mention it to Mike Smith the next time I see him," then email your contact in a day or two, reminding him or her to keep you in mind when they next speak with Mike Smith. You may not be able to control whether or not your contact follows through, but a note thanking him or her will help keep you in mind.

Be persistent

Even in the strongest economic booms, there will always be fierce competition for any job in the fashion industry. You may have to go through the above steps many times over several months before you are offered an interview. However, be persistent. This is the field in which you want to work. You've dedicated four challenging years to your education in the field. Remember your long-term goal, and always keep trying.

Job listings: Overt and covert

In general, job listings will fall into two distinct categories, as follows:

Overt job listings
Search online and in trade publications for job listings related to the fashion industry. Sites such as FashionJobs, StyleCareers, and Fashion.net are just three of the many resources available. Search the employment/careers section of the websites for your "best, better, good" list of employers. Often, jobs are listed on corporate Internet sites, but not on general job boards. *Women's Wear Daily* (wwd. com) is the industry standard for fashion industry news, and the publication also includes job listings.

Covert job listings
Many jobs aren't posted anywhere that a general search will be able to access, or aren't posted at all. These are positions that have recently become vacant because of a promotion, resignation, or reassignment. Clues as to where these jobs can be found lie in the news sections of industry websites and trade publications. Additionally, always keep your eyes and ears open. If you overhear someone mention that his or her friend, who was an assistant to a designer at a particular company recently got promoted or is moving on, consider writing a cover letter that same day to the Director of HR.

Internships and interviews:
At the interview

- **LEARN HOW TO PREPARE FOR AN INTERVIEW**
- **LEARN KEY TECHNIQUES FOR A SUCCESSFUL INTERVIEW**

Success in an interview depends on following some simple rules to demonstrate your strengths, while also presenting yourself as a professional and desirable candidate.

Many job seekers believe that all of the information about a company can be gleaned from reading the job description. This is incorrect and will automatically make you appear unprepared. Resources for learning more about a particular company include the Internet; trade publications such as *Women's Wear Daily*; and friends, teachers, mentors, or other acquaintances who know about the industry or, better yet, the company in question. Revealing a deep level of knowledge about the company will effectively convey your seriousness about the position to an interviewer.

Have your answers ready in advance

Many resources provide advice on which questions most often come up in interviews, as well as which ones are the most challenging to answer. Identify difficult interview questions and write out your answers to them. Then, refine your answers on paper and say them out loud in front of a mirror or, better still, role-play the interview questions with a friend. You want to sound polished, professional, and prepared, but not like someone reading from a script.

What to research about a company

You must always research a company thoroughly before the interview by identifying the following:

1 The company's key strengths and weaknesses.

2 Where the company is placed in the market relative to its competition.

3 Any recent announcements or product launches.

4 What the company's corporate culture is like (this is often revealed by the website's aesthetic).

5 The company's history, particularly in the past three years.

Checklist: A successful interview

- Have you done thorough research on the company before the interview?
- Have you identified typical interview questions and devised answers for them?
- Have you rehearsed your answers in advance?
- Have you planned your route and travel arrangements carefully to ensure that you arrive on time?
- Have you considered the impact your appearance, speech, and body language will have?
- Have you been truthful at all times during the interview?
- Are you ready to display a positive, enthusiastic attitude?
- Have you followed up your interview with a thank-you note?

Interview protocol

Most interviews will probably follow a typical pattern. Try to bear the following key points in mind when attending an interview:

Try to make small talk

Small talk is a critical part of the opening of an interview. It works as an icebreaker, demonstrates your social skills, and makes you feel less nervous because you have to focus on the conversation. Topics relating to the weather or an industry event, a compliment on how nice the building is, or a comment on a new product are just some of the topics that you can discuss during the first few minutes. Always make sure your small talk is about something neutral that you can discuss in a positive light.

Put the interviewer at ease

It is worth remembering that you may not be the only one who is nervous. The interviewer may also be nervous about meeting new people, so try to put the interviewer at ease as well. This will also help you to relax because you are establishing a friendly contact, while gaining some control over the situation.

Prove that you will fit in

Your résumé has shown the interviewer that you have the qualifications for the job. The interview enables the employer to identify two things: firstly, if what you said in your résumé is true and, secondly, if you'd fit in with the group you'll be working for and the company as a whole.

Looks, speech, and body language

There are three areas of presentation that will be noted: your physical appearance, your words, and your behavior. Within the first 10 seconds, every person you meet will form an impression of you. Be aware that each of these people, from the receptionist to the design director, may influence whether or not you're offered the job, so treat everyone with the utmost respect.

Maintain eye contact

During your interview, always maintain eye contact with the interviewer. This can be difficult if you're being interviewed in a busy office or you're facing an interviewer who has a lot of activity going on behind him or her. Ignore it all and focus on the person with whom you're speaking.

Always be honest

Be truthful at all times, even when you're trying to answer a difficult question. This is where your preparation comes in most useful: if you're prepared to answer a tough question, you will be able to look your interviewer in the eye and provide an honest answer. This will go a long way in impressing the interviewer. Conversely, never lie. Deception will always come out, either in your body language, a change in the tone of your voice, the pace at which you speak, or outside the interview during the background check that employers may perform before making an offer.

Stay optimistic

Always sound upbeat and enthusiastic. For instance, when asked about your most recent job, only talk about the good points, even if it was a negative experience.

Successful personal presentation

When being interviewed, always make sure that you:

1 Wear clean, well-pressed or steamed clothes.

2 Dress appropriately for the company and position for which you're interviewing. For example, if you are interviewing for the Gap, avoid wearing Chanel.

3 Prepare a few icebreakers for initial small talk.

4 Arrive early to the appointment; 10 minutes is the rule of thumb.

5 Briefly but sincerely apologize for your delay if you arrive late, and thank them for their patience in waiting. Only apologize at the start, and then never mention it again because you don't want to remind them in case they forget over the course of the interview!

6 Walk in the door with a positive attitude. It will show in your words and how you carry yourself physically during the interview.

7 Smile and look people in the eye. Even if you're nervous, don't avoid eye contact.

8 Always shake hands with each person to whom you are introduced.

9 Repeat back each person's name after he or she says it, such as, "It's a pleasure to meet you, John," if you have trouble remembering names.

10 Always say thank you to everyone—not just to the interviewer, but also to the receptionist who helped guide you to your seat, the staffer who offered you a glass of water, and so on.

After the interview

On leaving, thank interviewers for their time, shake hands, and smile (while still maintaining eye contact). Within a day, send interviewers a handwritten note to thank them again, and make sure you reiterate your interest in the job. Additionally, if you have any questions you wanted to ask, but didn't think of during the interview, include these in the note. It will help emphasize your interest in the job and may also prompt more dialog with interviewers, something that usually helps distinguish you from the competition.

If a week goes by and you haven't heard anything back from the company, contact interviewers to check in and ask if there's been any movement in the hiring process, or if there's anything else they need from you in their consideration of your application. Ideally, speak directly with the interviewer. If necessary, you can leave a voicemail message for him or her, but make sure you state your name and phone number twice—once at the beginning of the message and once at the end—and speak slowly enough so that the interviewer can write the phone number down easily.

If you don't receive a response, be patient and don't call back. There are an infinite number of reasons why they may not get back to you, but, no matter what the reason, they may perceive you as being too aggressive if you persist in calling.

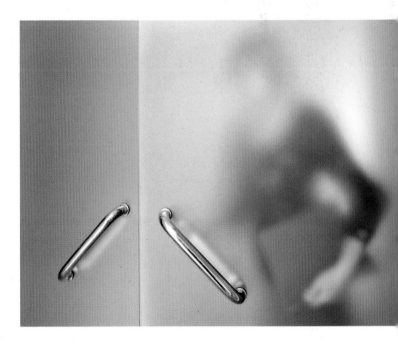

In the workplace

- **HOW TO GET AHEAD**
- **BUILDING PRODUCTIVE RELATIONSHIPS**

Learning how to navigate the working environment is critical to success, along with talent and a positive, professional attitude.

Working with others

Unfortunately, the modern workplace is not always a collaborative, trust-filled environment. Always focus on your own goals—both short- and long-term—in order to protect your best interests from more predatory colleagues. Some important points to bear in mind are:

1 The importance of temperament
Never, ever be anything less than cordial, polite, and upbeat. People may not remember every good thing you do for them, but they will remember every negative thing you do. Always greet colleagues in a polite manner, thank them for their help, and never speak ill of colleagues, superiors, or assistants. The same goes for email and IM correspondence: always maintain a positive, respectful, and professional demeanor.

2 Reading body language
As in an interview, body language often reveals more about a situation than the words exchanged. In the daily work environment, keep tabs on the body language of the people with whom you interact. Does your manager cross her arms every time you speak? If so, she may feel defensive. Is your colleague friendly, but rarely makes eye contact? If so, there may be deceit on his side of the relationship. When you read body language, you gain insights into where the other person is coming from and what's important to him or her. By understanding this, you are in a strong position to determine how you will respond to him or her, which can be an invaluable tool in diffusing a tense situation or assuring your manager that you are not after his or her job.

3 The value of respect
When you are first introduced to someone, make sure that you remember his or her name, but more importantly make a mental note of how the person prefers to be addressed. Twenty years ago, it was common to refer to colleagues and superiors as, say, Mr. Brown or Ms. White. Today, the convention in most professional environments is to refer to someone by the first name. This rule generally holds true, but for two exceptions. Firstly, if the

The golden rule for being a professional

No matter what you do, no matter what stage you are at in your career, **treat everyone you meet with respect, consideration, and civility.** Never gossip, back talk, or disrespect your colleagues. Fashion, although it is a global industry, is also a very insular one. The people you step on at the beginning of your career may end up determining your future success or failure at some stage later on.

Checklist: Good office behavior

- Are you keeping your career goals in mind in all your work dealings?
- Are you perfectly polite and respectful at all times?
- Are you aware of the body language of your colleagues?
- Do you use the right terms of address for different colleagues?
- Do you avoid office gossip at all costs?
- Are you adopting a positive or at least neutral stance each day?
- Do you treat others how you would wish to be treated?
- Do you treat all members of staff with the same degree of respect?

person who has introduced you refers to the other person as "Mr." or "Ms." (and is not corrected in any way), then you will need to wait for an invitation from that person to call him or her by a first name. Secondly, never refer to people by a nickname, unless they have expressly asked you to do so. People can be sensitive about names, and overstepping the boundaries of familiarity can be costly, both to your relationships and your success in that job.

4 Never, ever gossip
In every workplace, in every company, in every industry, people gossip about others. As a new colleague, you'll be drawn into these conversations with your coworkers. It is essential that you consistently maintain either a neutral or positive

public stance on your opinion of all your coworkers at every level. If you say something negative about another person, you can guarantee it will get back to him or her before the end of the day. And, most likely, the version he or she will hear is far worse than what you've said. It's much easier to keep quiet as others gossip than to have to apologize for your own slip-of-the-tongue.

2 rules for dealing with other people

In fashion, as in any other profession, there are two rules that should guide your words and actions on the job:

1 Treat others how you wish to be treated.

2 Never put in writing anything you don't want the whole world to know.

These tried and true adages have saved many people from workplace disaster. Unfortunately, the many people who haven't adhered to them have suffered irreparable damage to their careers.

Careers in fashion

Fashion design encompasses a tremendous array of skills that relate to nearly every area of the industry. What may appear as disparate elements operating within their own area is actually a highly choreographed system that chain-reacts to produce a collection every season.

Listed on the following pages are careers that all work together in order to create fashion.

Head designer/design director

At the top of the design room pyramid is the head designer and/or design director. For companies such as Donna Karan, this would include Ms. Karan, as well as her design director. For other companies, this may simply be the company's founder. As the creative leaders, they decide on the general mood and direction for the upcoming season and work very closely with their designers. They'll volley ideas around with the design team, while ultimately serving as a coach and editor for what the design team proposes, always making sure that the team is on track. In extremely large companies, this area of hierarchy might also include vice presidents and senior vice presidents of design. The head designer/design director typically reports to the business owner or CEO.

Designer

Designers are the creative voice of a collection. They are typically the team members who are the first to generate the inspirations and design development, create the fabric and color stories, perform huge amounts of trend and market research, and ultimately provide the design director with a well-merchandised collection. They oversee everything from top to bottom before the

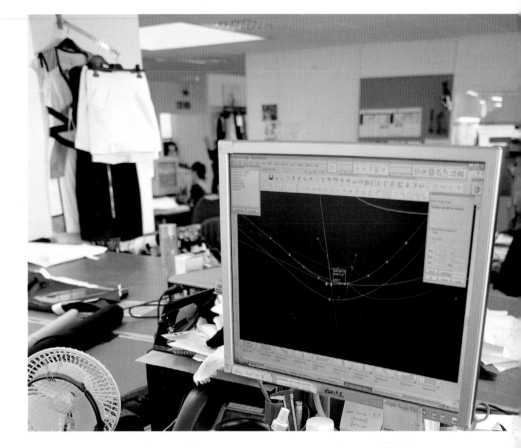

design director gives final approval. Although the potential for creativity is high, designers who work for a large corporate company such as J. Crew or Abercrombie & Fitch have many people above them who give them a design lead that they must follow every season.

Assistant and associate designer

As entry-level positions, assistant and associate designers are responsible for doing whatever the designer throws their way. For some companies, particularly larger ones, this may include photocopying, administrative work, submitting orders for trims and fabric, flat-sketching, finalizing mood boards, performing market research, working with the sample room, and making sure everything runs efficiently. In smaller operations, in which the design teams are intimate and the hierarchy shorter, the responsibilities may include design work, fabric sourcing, inspiration research, trips to international factories, visiting fabric fairs such as Première Vision, print design and other forms of textile development, and further creative responsibilities. Assistant and associate positions usually last between one and three years before promotion to the next level.

CAD operator/designer (computer-aided design)

CAD operators work in one or two ways: either as designers who work alongside the design team and create prints,

knit designs, and stripe layouts, or as technicians who digitally execute work that has been designed for them. They may work as part of the in-house team or as external freelancers who are hired during presentation deadlines, or when the collection is entering the production phase and packages need to be sent to factories. The work often includes tasks such as producing digital flats and illustrations, print and textile designs, technical knit designs, and graphic designs for printed collateral, and preparing specification packages for factories where garment measurements are provided for production.

Fabric research and development

A true luxury for some design houses is the addition of a fabric research and development department. Although many companies resource their fabrics externally, some teams develop their own in-house fabrications as a signature of the brand. In addition to fabric development, associates are expected to resource and order yardage, and have

it transported to the company's various international factories on time, particularly during the production season. They may visit fabric mills to view the latest line and make special requests for development, resource specific fabric types that their designers are seeking and barter for the best price, and work with mills to discuss future trends. For those companies that resource fabric externally, fabric suppliers have their own showroom representatives in major fashion capitals that show the latest season's offerings and place the designer's orders.

Sales and showroom representative

Sales and showroom representatives are responsible for showing the new line to press and store buyers. As a representative of the company, they must not only possess excellent sales skills, but also represent the company's image in the best possible way. They work closely with the designers upon the completion of the line, so they understand how to articulate the collection's inspiration, fabric choices, design direction, and overall message. They may also work with the design team before the next collection begins in order to review previous sales figures so that the designers understand where to continue, particularly if an item did exceptionally well. Sales representatives can be a strong feature of a company's success because they are expected to form close, personal relationships with powerful store buyers.

Production manager

Production managers are the unsung heroes of a fashion design operation. Once a collection is finished and store orders are placed, their job truly begins. Production managers ensure that the collection is made in a timely manner and within strict quality guidelines. They oversee the sample room's pattern makers and seamstresses, order vast quantities of fabric and have it delivered to the correct mills on a tight schedule, secure trims and notions for delivery at the same time as the fabric, meet with factories to negotiate production prices, review samples for quality standards, ensure that garments receive proper labeling, and organize the shipment of produced garments to the stores.

Managers are highly organized and orchestrated people who work on a global level; it is not uncommon to time a two-week fabric delivery from Europe to a factory in Asia so that it does not sit for more than two days before being cut and sewn because of limited storage space.

Pattern maker/draper/sample hand

As the team who brings the designer's vision to life, the sample hands are invaluable. They are often experts with not only a deep level of skill, but also a tremendous grasp of the designer's aesthetic. For this reason, it is not uncommon for such reputable houses to have a highly loyal team that has been with the company since its inception. Their ability to create garments that fit exceptionally well can boost sales exponentially, or create a disaster if the fit is less than perfect for the customer. The "3-D Team" must also have an excellent understanding of fabric, as particularities will determine the best methods of execution in draping, sewing, and pattern making.

Retail buyer

Buyers have one of the most glamorous and the most daunting of all jobs. From visiting designer's studios for previews, sitting in the audience during runway shows, predicting upcoming trends their customers will respond to, and deciding what merchandise will ultimately fill the sales floor and give a cohesive point-of-view, a buyer must make the right choices in order to sustain the business. Failure to do so can mean catastrophe. Buyers must be attuned not only to fashion, but also to other aspects of consumer psychology and the greater cultural barometer. How things trickle up or down from the unlikeliest of places cannot be overlooked, given just how sensitive and fickle the consumer environment can be.

Retail manager

From such large corporations as Macy's and Selfridges to the more exclusive and intimate environments of a designer's boutique, the retail manager ensures that daily operations run smoothly, while also planning for long-term initiatives such as launching new collections, scheduling designer trunk shows, hiring and training staff, generating merchandising and sales reports, forward planning, and creating store presentations. They are responsible for meeting the company's sales goals, while also serving as the key

disseminators of information to their sales teams about the new merchandise. One of the most important areas of the manager's job is to ensure that the sales team is motivated and well trained, and receives support in areas such as performance reviews and scheduling.

Sales associate

The types of associates that work in a retail environment are as diverse as the types of venues themselves. However, as representatives of the store and its image, they are expected to service customers and fully understand the merchandise they are selling in order to best communicate aspects that may not be obvious. These aspects could range from the collection's theme, details about garment construction and finishing, fabric and laundering knowledge, and even how alterations can best be performed. In the designer's own boutiques, associates often keep files on their frequent customers in order to develop long-term relationships. They'll pull looks together and call in their customers, arrange all fittings and delivery of merchandise, send personal thank-you notes and birthday cards, and may even act as their personal stylist!

Fashion journalist

Fashion journalists serve as news agents and critics of fashion, particularly during collections week. As news agents, they offer us views into designer studios, discuss the current trends, and provide information for what is happening in the fashion industry. As critics, they review collections each season and analyze how the work serves as a barometer for the shifting cultural climate. A successful critic understands the history of each designer's work and is able to put the current collection in this context, while also absorbing the elements shown across the current season. Regardless of the area, a journalist's job never stops, particularly in fashion, where the emphasis is always on what's next. Trade publications that are published daily, such as *Women's Wear Daily*, offer the most up-to-date information.

Costume historian

As a relatively new field, the study of fashion history has been given great attention by such leading institutions as The Metropolitan Museum of Art in New York and the Victoria and Albert Museum in London. Fashion makes profound reflections on culture, and it is the historian's responsibility to articulate this through visual and written means. From such forms of dissemination as gallery exhibitions, articles published in academic journals, and biographies about designers and their particular time period, a costume historian researches fashion as a cultural and meaningful artifact. A graduate degree is generally required, and positions are frequently found in museums, galleries, academia, and auction houses or as research assistants and freelance writers.

Print/textile/surface designer

Virtually every fashion brand uses print or graphic design work in their collections. A fashion graduate who specializes or has an affinity for this area may find work within a fashion brand's design room or another agency specializing in prints. As a specialist in this field, the areas for product development are endless and include textiles for fashion and interiors and paper goods such as wallpaper and home decor. Work is primarily computer-generated, and a deep understanding of color, environment, product usage, and customer profile is needed. Designers often work as a service and within a predetermined direction, as set by their customers.

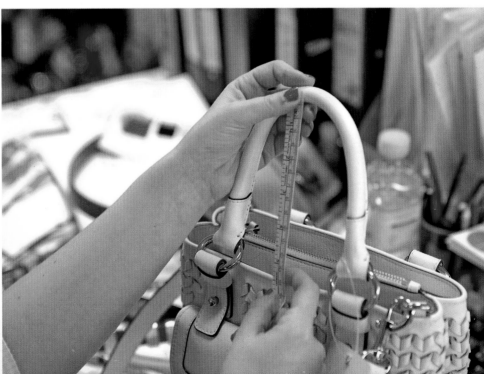

Accessory designer

Accessory designers are sculptors who make products that are used for purely aesthetic and/or utilitarian purposes. They can work as designers who offer accessories only, such as Manolo Blahnik or Jimmy Choo; for a large house such as Ralph Lauren or Jil Sander, where accessories simply complement the highly emphasized clothing; or for houses such as Gucci and Nike that offer accessories in equal emphasis to their clothing lines. Designers who gravitate to this area are often those who enjoy the engineering and ergonomics of design, while using an almost limitless source of materials. Although many brands may be based on familiar silhouettes and what has succeeded at retail, working with accessories allows for unbridled creativity through product development.

Costume designer

Costume design is often separated into two distinct areas: movies and theater. Both areas require a deep understanding of how color, fabric, texture, construction, and even a garment's movement create a visual impression of a character. All forms of fashion design are nonverbal communications about the wearer, and theatrical costume is an even greater representation of this.

Costume designers must be highly attuned not only to the story and each character's personality, but also to historical costume design, period construction methods, lighting, and the other elements of production that may affect how color and fabric are perceived by an audience.

Stylist

Stylists create a vision. Whether they work alongside a designer to create a dynamic runway show, produce editorial layouts for fashion publications, or work with celebrities and other clients to perfect their public personas, stylists have an innate grasp of how to realize and cultivate a unique point of view in fashion presentation. Stylists are often referred to as fashion editors, artistic directors, creative directors, and personal shoppers. Some styling talents, such as Grace Coddington with *Vogue*, Melanie Ward with Helmut Lang, and Katie Grand with Alexander McQueen, have become legendary. Stylists are responsible for generating the desired image, as requested by their client.

Public relations

Public relations specialists communicate to the public on behalf of the company. They control the amount of information given to the public and always aim to present information in the best possible light and through the most appropriate channel. They must be highly articulate in written material and in verbal presentation when managing information through such media vehicles as press releases, website content, conferences, exhibitions, benefits, and fashion shows. Their ultimate goal is to raise awareness of the brand, to garner the right kind of media coverage, and to strategically build the company through short- and long-term planning. As a public persona, you are expected to represent the brand in the best possible way at all times, and to be outgoing and persistent in order to get your brand noticed!

Trend forecasting

As perhaps the ultimate consumer of all information related to fashion, trend forecasters have a sixth sense for what's to come, based on research and intuition. They must be fully immersed in all facets of the world's cultural landscape—from both local and global perspectives—because of the ripple effect that can occur and thus shift consumer behavior. Their trend reporting can range from color, fabric, silhouette, lifestyle, and general approach to fashion consumption that is either currently being demonstrated in the market or for where and how we are evolving.

Agencies such as Li Edelkoort's Trend Union that make predictions about where fashion is heading are subscribed to by fabric mills, designers, and retailers in order to help them strategize future business plans.

Event planning/show production

Event planners are typically freelance agencies that work for brands to produce press events such as fashion shows. Their expertise centers on staging, rentals, lighting design, sound systems, catering, interior design, space layout, and the host of other concerns that need to be addressed when putting on a large-scale production. Event producers can also be instrumental in acquiring necessary licenses or permits, along with ensuring that safety codes are met. The fashion world is just one area where event planners use their skills in organizing runway shows, conferences, benefit galas, charity events, auctions, award ceremonies, and many other unique opportunities.

Fashion illustrator

Despite the passing heyday of fashion illustration as an advertising tool, there has been a resurgence of interest in fashion illustration. Fashion designers may hire freelance illustrators to depict the mood and silhouettes of the collection during the editing process and before sample production. Illustrators are also hired as freelancers for advertising campaigns, editorial work, teachers, and other forms of media.

Fashion photographer

Like fashion illustrators, a photographer's role is to bring the fashion being documented onto a higher plane. For those creating editorial work for magazines, a direction is often provided by fashion editors that photographers must then follow, while also using their own creative license. The field can be glamorous and creatively rewarding, though highly competitive. Other forms of fashion photography include catalog work that often relies on direct shots of the product being sold. Photographers must possess a vast array of skills, including the highly technical and creative, as well as the ability to connect with models in order to generate the best possible work.

Graphic designer

The world of graphic design is seemingly limitless, and there are few other professional areas that offer such a high degree of creative license than that of fashion. As people who work with words, media, and images, graphic designers must be highly attuned to how a viewer acquires knowledge. Using a strong understanding of design principles, such as line, color, shape, and composition, graphic designers take a concept to create fashion design collateral such as brochures, logos, garment hang tags, business cards, show invitations, posters, and even websites. Their work can have a profound impact on a company's image and brand, as seen with such iconic examples as "Tiffany Blue" and "Hermès Orange," Chanel's entwined "C" logo, and the iconic swoosh used by Nike.

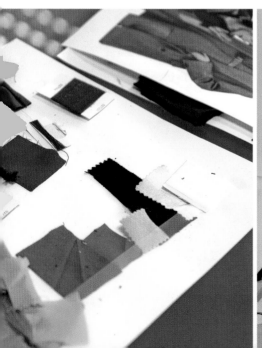

Interview: From student to designer

Lisa Mayock and Sophie Buhai

Designers, Vena Cava

Lisa Mayock and Sophie Buhai graduated from Parsons The New School for Design in 2003. Following their graduation, the two collaborated on a collection that was shown during New York Fashion Week. They have been nominated twice for the coveted CFDA/Vogue Fashion Fund Award, and in 2009 they were runners-up for the Fashion Finalist Fund. Lisa and Sophie have collaborated with brands such as the Gap and Converse. The Vena Cava collection is carried at top retailers such as Saks Fifth Avenue, Opening Ceremony, and Bergdorf Goodman.

What was the biggest surprise for you leaving school and entering the professional world?

Lisa Mayock: The biggest surprise was how much I thought I knew when I graduated—and then shortly thereafter realizing that I had so much to learn! I felt like I had a good handle on aspects of design; how to design a cohesive collection—how to illustrate that collection, make technical drawings and construct it—but very little real-world application of those ideas. I was totally unfamiliar with most stores besides department stores; I had no concept of branding or creating an identity, or marketing myself—I just knew what I liked. Which in the end became my brand.

Sophie Buhai: Business! We had learned design in school, but we had no idea about profit margins, sales terms, and overheads. I ended up taking a few business classes so that I could better understand what we were getting into. I made a lot of mistakes and had to learn how to manage finances. Because we were starting our business from nothing, I cared a lot about making ends meet, and thus business became very interesting and crucial to our growth and survival.

Reflecting back on your years at school, what do you wish you did more/less of?

LM: I wish I had a better understanding of the real business of fashion. I will admit that I wasn't the most attentive student in our business class, but in hindsight I wish there were more mandatory business classes, and mandatory fashion history classes. I spend a lot more time researching for my collections now, whether in the library, at a museum, or at certain stores. Being a designer means you have to know what else exists out there, and how you can do it better.

MATTER-OF-FACT MEMPHIS
Vena Cava's belief in accessible and functional fashion design is evident in this spring/summer collection inspired by the 1980s' Memphis design movement. As classmates, Mayock and Buhai developed their shared design philosophy that ultimately led them to launch their brand immediately following their education at Parsons.

Is there particular advice you would give to students who are in their final year?

LM: Get an internship! In fact, get a few. There is no better way to know what you want (or even more importantly, what you don't want) than to experience it and see for yourself. If you want to have your own small business, I recommend interning at one or two small design houses, and then intern at a large company. What you end up gravitating toward could be very different than you first expected. This is also the best way to learn about the real business and the issues that designers experience every day.

SB: Really figure out what your style is and what makes your aesthetic different from others. Are you offering something new? Make sure your work is honest and true to who you are.

What are the hallmarks of "good" design?

LM: Good design is both functional and beautiful. It can make your eye feel like it's finally resting upon the right thing, or it can feel totally jarring, weird, and foreign. A lot of things I love I thought looked strange the first time I saw them. It turns out it was my eye getting used to something new.

SB: For me it's wearability. If you can make something that is functional and subtly unique, then you're really solving a problem. The biggest compliment we get is when a woman says she has worn a dress of ours over and over again for years. I like the idea of designing heirlooms; to me that is sentimental and sustainable.

What makes a successful portfolio?

LM: One that doesn't look like everyone else's. If you can find a way to really "brand" yourself and bring that into your portfolio, you will be the one that potential employers remember. Think about your aesthetic and apply that to your portfolio. Are you a box person or a book person? Or is it another format altogether? What materials do you gravitate toward? When I see portfolios that are executed well—truly unique in presentation as well as design—that's someone I see as having great potential because they consider every detail.

What is the best aspect of owning your own label?

LM: The best and worst part of owning your own label is being your own boss. Getting to create your own methods for how to operate, manage, and run a business can be thrilling and rewarding, and it feels good to be able to dream up something and create it. However, not having anyone in charge can be difficult. We've never had an investor or someone who runs any part of our business. We've learned to do it all ourselves. It's something I'm very proud of, but on some days it would be great to have someone tell you what to do, do it, go home, and not think about work 24 hours a day.

What are the biggest challenges or surprises?

LM: The challenges have changed continuously along the way. At first it was getting people to pay attention, then it was giving them a reason to keep paying attention. Finding ways to keep it exciting and fresh can be hard in a business that runs on such short deadlines. What it boils down to is that if you truly love and are excited about what you do, other people will be too. Your product should excite you as much as the people buying it.

Interview: Focus on key points

Steven Kolb

Executive Director, Council of Fashion Designers of America

As Executive Director of the Council of Fashion Designers of America, Steven oversees all operations and activities of the American fashion industry's preeminent designer trade association and affiliated charity. Membership consists of more than 370 of America's leading apparel and accessories designers. His responsibilities include all member services, trade association activities, and philanthropic initiatives. He reports to and works directly with Board President Diane von Furstenberg and the board comprising 27 of America's foremost designers.

How has the fashion industry evolved in the past five years? What are the key areas and reasons for the change?

Fashion has become more democratic. Designers are working at every price point and in multiple categories. The idea that fashion is only at designer level has changed. There has been growth in the contemporary market and in the market between contemporary and designer. I believe technology has changed fashion. Consumers are more intimately aware of fashion and the people who work in fashion—the personality of a designer is important and drives a brand's image. There has been tremendous growth in pre-fall and resort collections, and many designers are delivering product every month to retail. Also, fashion is now a global business and designers must be keenly aware of international markets and their potential. The traditional channels of distribution are not enough any more: the future of shopping is e-commerce.

What are your views on fashion education today? Are there areas that need greater focus when training the new generation of designers?

Education is important no matter what the field. Having just an idea or creative vision is not enough and will get you nowhere. Studying fashion is important because it gives an aspiring designer the detailed practices and specific tools needed to execute an idea. I think fashion schools need to have a core focus on the fundamentals. It is important to know how to sketch, sew, drape, and to have knowledge of pattern making. Business education is equally important. Most designers start a business by themselves, and need to have strong management skills and business acumen. There should be more emphasis on the history of fashion—there is so much

FASHION FETE
With a membership consisting of more than 370 of America's foremost designers, the CFDA leads industry-wide initiatives that include the annual CFDA Fashion Awards, scholarship awards for students, and professional development for young designers.

to learn from the techniques and past collections of other designers.

What are the "ideal" attributes a graduate must possess when entering the professional field?

The most successful graduates are organized and have a plan. They know what they want to do or who they want to work for. Confidence is a key attribute. Believing in yourself is important, as is being grounded and humble with talent and past successes. Take your time. An ability to work closely with others and to respect the opinions and ideas of others is needed.

How can fashion students make the most of their undergraduate years?

Practical work time in the studio is important. Students should take advantage of intern opportunities. The experience of being around working designers, no matter what the task, can give students a foundation to build from when they begin working. It is also important to be familiar with the industry. Reading industry publications and knowing what the current fashion landscape is can frame a student's perspective. There are many opportunities to volunteer at industry events, which is a good way to meet people and to see firsthand how things happen.

How would you describe a successful portfolio? What are the hallmarks?

A successful portfolio is well organized, clear, and simple; not over the top, but to the point, and clearly representative of the designer. The overall portfolio inside and out is important, but avoid too much "presentation" on the outside of the portfolio, and keep the main focus on the information on the inside, keeping in mind that the whole package works together. It should represent your best body of work and should be edited and precise; no one wants to see everything you ever did.

What makes a successful designer or brand?

Having a point of view and owning it is important. A successful designer has their core and is known for that. The core is never abandoned and the designer grows his or her success by building out from the core. Knowing the customer is equally important. The end result should be to sell: creation without commerce is not fashion.

Will the role of the future fashion designer change?

An idea always starts within the brain of the designer, so that will never change. I think the change is not with the designer or the creator, but with how garments or accessories are manufactured and sold. A designer needs to be aware of that change. Types of material, cleaner manufacturing, new ways to sell, and changing deliveries will impact creativity.

Interview: Global design

Dan Rubinstein

Editor-in-Chief, *Surface* magazine

Dan Rubinstein is a design writer, editor, and curator, and is Editor-in-Chief of *Surface* magazine. He was also a staffer at *House & Garden* and has contributed to publications such as *O at Home*, *The New York Times Style Magazine*, *Out*, *Architectural Record*, *Slate*, and many others. His series of public programs on contemporary American furniture, "The Home Front," was recently completed at the Museum of Arts and Design (MAD). Rubinstein lives and works in New York.

What has occurred in design over the past five years, and why?

I cover design from multiple angles: fashion, furniture, architecture, product, and everything in between. In doing so, I have a unique viewpoint that's focused more on the design end of things than on the commercial end. When it comes to the last five years in the design world, there are a few overriding influences that I've noticed. First is how the global "crisis" (or recession, if you'd prefer) has impacted the output of design, both on the creative and commercial ends of the spectrum. When I first joined *Surface*, money was flowing and a lot of emerging design relied heavily on new technologies, one-off pieces of unwearable/unusable work, and the like. I've definitely seen a return to traditional craft, an appreciation of the subtle use of materials, and wearability. New labels aren't looking to shock any more; they're looking to survive. Yes, in some ways they're taking less risks, but the output seems to be more considered and of a higher quality. Only the best survives.

How has the design industry evolved in the past five to seven years?

That's hard to say. On the media side of things in fashion, there's been a huge shift in terms of the acceptance of the digital world and e-commerce. Many brands wouldn't have been caught dead advertising or selling online just a few years ago. But now that's all changed, and continues to do so. Many brands now rely on online sources of income. When sites such as Gilt Groupe are raking in hundreds of millions of dollars in sales each year—mostly from "designer" fashion products that are made especially for their flash sales—that's bound to have an impact, whether the industry's old guard is willing to admit to it or not. It's bound to have an

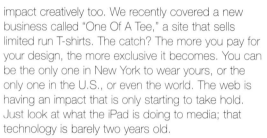

impact creatively too. We recently covered a new business called "One Of A Tee," a site that sells limited run T-shirts. The catch? The more you pay for your design, the more exclusive it becomes. You can be the only one in New York to wear yours, or the only one in the U.S., or even the world. The web is having an impact that is only starting to take hold. Just look at what the iPad is doing to media; that technology is barely two years old.

When you look at the globalization of design, how do the industries differ and how are they similar?

The globalization of design is happening faster and faster than ever before. The web, of course, is accelerating that trend in the ways we consume media and information, as well as e-commerce. Also, students are traveling farther than ever before for a design education. Countries in Asia are sending their students to Europe and the U.S. by the thousands. Many will stay, and many more will go home and take their creative spirits with them. It's also hard to forget the impact that the E.U. has had in all of this. We joke around the office that nearly every designer we profile is described as something like an "Indonesian-born, French-raised, London-schooled, Brooklyn-based talent who splits his time between New York and Tokyo…" It's becoming the norm. You'd think that globalization is making everything creatively similar, but in fact, people have to be more unique than ever to stand out in the crowd, especially in cyberspace.

What do students need to understand (or learn) most?

That they live in a global design community where, in many cases, only the globetrotting entrepreneur can survive. Provincial thinkers are doomed from the start.

How can students make the most of their final year in an undergraduate program?

Every young designer is their own brand, even if they're working a day job at the Gap. First, you should be interning not just in your senior year, but beginning in your freshman year to build your contacts. Never meet anyone without taking his or her business card. Stay in touch with everyone you know. Also, being your own brand, you should know everything there is to know about the presentation and marketing of your work, from photography to PR. I think every young designer should intern for a big fashion PR agency or publication, at one point or another. Then, consider a higher education abroad, preferably in a country you've never been to. Network with other students or early professionals in graphic design or photography so your look book or website is 100 percent professional. Develop a capsule collection; it doesn't matter if you make five of each piece that are sold in just one boutique or just online. It's a calling card, and the web lets any one-man-band seem legit. Globalization is turning everyone into entrepreneurs, so no one should leave school without a firm grasp of how the market works, and the value of meticulous presentation. Myspace pages just won't cut it any more.

INNOVATION ARENA
As a leader in showcasing the forefront of design, *Surface* magazine highlights well-established and young designers from around the world who are bringing innovation to fashion design. Other featured disciplines, such as architecture and furniture design, give readers a deeper and more contextualized understanding of global design and how the world's aesthetic is evolving.

Interview: Developing as a designer

Matthew Ames

Designer, Matthew Ames

After earning a BFA from the School of the Art Institute of Chicago in 2003, Matthew worked for Jurgi Persoons in Antwerp, Belgium, and Miguel Adrover in New York. In 2004, he was the first American finalist for the Festival de la Mode à Hyères in France. Ames presented his first collection in 2005 and in 2009 received the 8th annual Ecco Domani Fashion Foundation Award. In 2010, he was a finalist for The Fashion Group International Rising Star Award and was recognized by *Vogue* as one of the "new guard" of American fashion designers.

What advice would you give to students in their final year of study?

It's important to start focusing on creating your own world and identity as a designer and to go deep into that world. It's the only time you have in your career to be completely free and not have to worry about commercial and other pressures that arise once you start working within the industry system. I recommend that students try to remove themselves from looking at the current trends in the industry and what other designers are doing; they will create work that is more pure, innovative, and exciting. It's easy for students today to go online and look at all the collections each season, but it can become dangerous. I see a lot of student work that is clearly too influenced by other collections or designers. Students should ask themselves, "Why am I creating this shape and is it because I saw so and so designer do it last season?" Spend more time looking at actual clothes and studying the ideas and construction behind them as opposed to researching collections online. I would also recommend that students use their teachers as much as possible. They are your best resource when you're in school and they usually have more to share than what they teach in the classroom.

How would you describe your transition from school to profession?

After graduating from the School of the Art Institute of Chicago, I moved to New York and began working for the designer Miguel Adrover. I hadn't spent much time in New York before then and knew very little about how the industry worked. I think this benefited me and my work (when I started working on my own) because I was open to doing things in new ways and wasn't so inhibited by having to do things in the same way everyone else did them.

REDUCTIVE DESIGN
The clean, confident lines of Ames' work demonstrate a deep sensitivity for cut and proportion. Using superior quality fabrications and construction techniques are imperative when creating such deceptively simple design.

Working for Miguel Adrover was a huge learning experience for me. I came from a school that was about ideas and not so much about the fashion industry. The team there was small, so I was able to oversee everything from design and collection development to sales and marketing. Certainly, this helped me when I started my own label a couple of years later and I knew how to manage all of these different sides. Prior to working for Miguel, I spent time in Antwerp, Belgium, working with Jurgi Persoons. This opened me up to another side of fashion and was a big turning point. It made me think about clothes and not just ideas. I spent time working with Jurgi in Antwerp as well as Paris, so when I came to New York I had a more global understanding of the industry.

Where do you think fashion is headed and why?

The industry is at a crossroads. I don't think it has figured out the best way to use the current technology, speed, and accessibility of information. I hope that we start to see more designers working outside the established system of large seasonal collections and pre-collections, and photographing everything and putting it online six months before it's available in stores. This allows for knock-offs, lesser quality, and a less desirable product. There is too much disposable product being put out there and high-end designers need to focus on creating lasting pieces that are more directed to their customer.

What has been your biggest hurdle in being a designer?

When I started my label, I was showing it in Paris instead of New York. It was the natural progression for me as I had just shown my work at the Festival Hyères in France, but it was unusual at the time to have an American designer showing in Paris. People always want to put you in a box and the Europeans thought my collection was too American and the Americans thought it was too European. I've always thought my work is more connected with American fashion—in a traditional sense—but it didn't quite fit with the American trends at the time. However, there was support for what I was doing and showing in Paris, which gave me the space and time to develop and perfect the collection out of the spotlight. After a few seasons I started working with a showroom in New York and began introducing the collection there. In 2009, I was a recipient of the Ecco Domani Fashion Foundation Award and I felt the time was right for me to start showing during fashion week here. At that point, I had spent enough time developing the collection to present it to a larger audience, and people started to understand what my work is about and where it fits in the market.

How would you describe your creative process? How/why has it evolved?

Each season is an evolution of the previous one; it's not a new theme or concept, but it's about developing slowly and perfecting the ideas from one season to the next. My ideas about clean shapes and geometry were there at the beginning, but it was more about construction; it looked simple, but was a complicated process. Then I started stripping things down and removing everything from the clothes. I wanted to create a clean slate and a new framework for myself. From there, I started to build on those ideas. I usually have an idea for the silhouette, color, and fabric when I start working on a collection, but I begin by draping and working on the pattern. The collection develops from that.

Resources:
The fashion calendar

Fashion is now a global phenomenon, with an unprecedented interest in both fashion and design among consumers.

The concept of holding fashion weeks in only Paris, Milan, London, and New York is outdated—today's fashion industry is a truly global phenomenon. And with increased access to media, the possibilities for international exposure of talent is endless.

In addition to runway shows that showcase seasonal collections, festivals and fairs have long been a part of designers' annual agendas. Such events allow the fashion industry to research upcoming trends, view the latest offerings from fabric mills, and come together as a community in their own niche market to discuss their industry's future.

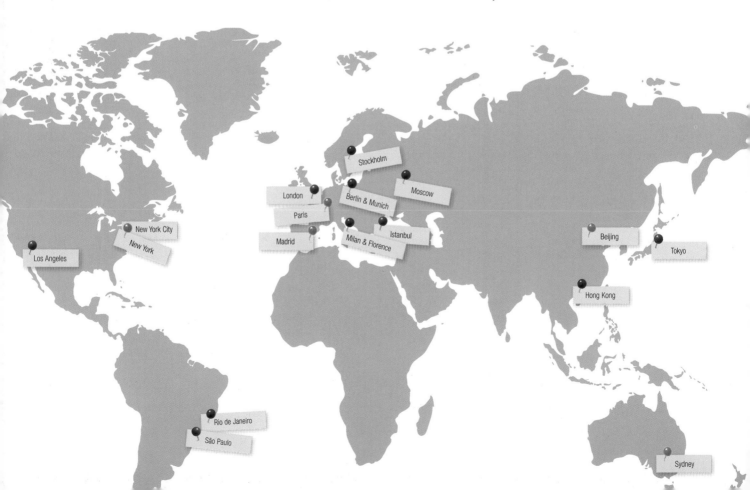

Important fashion events

Listed below are just some of the events and opportunities held around the world. Exact dates vary each year, but the majority of events are held at approximately the same time each month.

EVENT	DATE	LOCATION
Rio de Janeiro	Mid-January	Rio de Janeiro
Pitti Immagine Uomo	Mid-January	Florence
Hong Kong Fashion Week	Mid-January	Hong Kong
Berlin Fashion Week	Mid-January	Berlin
Milan Menswear	Mid-January	Milan
Paris Menswear	Late January	Paris
Pitti Immagine Bimbo	Late January	Florence
Paris Haute Couture	Late January	Paris
Paris Couture	Late January	Paris
Pitti Immagine Filati	Late January	Florence
São Paulo Women's RTW	Late January–early February	São Paulo
Stockholm Fashion Week	Late January–early February	Stockholm
Prato Expo	February	Milan
Première Vision	Early February	Paris
New York Women's RTW	Early–mid-February	New York
Paris Women's RTW	Early February–early March	Paris
London Women's RTW	Mid-February	London
Madrid Fashion Week	Mid-February	Madrid
Bridal Fashion Week	Mid-February	New York
Munich Fashion Week	Mid–late February	Munich
The Coterie	Late February	New York City
Milan Women's RTW	Late February–early March	Milan
Istanbul Fashion Fair	Early March	Istanbul

EVENT	DATE	LOCATION
Los Angeles Fashion Week	Mid-March	Los Angeles
Japan Fashion Week	Mid–late March	Tokyo
Première Vision Beijing	Late March–early April	Beijing
Russian Fashion Week	Late March–early April	Moscow
Sydney Fashion Week	Early May	Sydney
Los Angeles Fashion Market	Mid-June	Los Angeles
Pitti Immagine Uomo	Mid-June	Florence
Milan Menswear	Mid-June	Milan
Paris Menswear	Late June	Paris
Pitti Immagine Bimbo	Late June	Florence
Bread and Butter	July	Berlin
Pitti Immagine Filati	Early July	Florence
Haute Couture	Early July	Paris
Première Vision New York	Mid-July	New York
Prato Expo	September	Milan
New York Women's RTW	Early–mid-September	New York
London Women's RTW	Mid-September	London
Première Vision	Late September	Paris
Milan Women's RTW	Late September	Milan
Madrid Fashion Week	Late September	Madrid
Paris Women's RTW	Late September–early October	Paris
Russian Fashion Week	Mid-October	Moscow
Los Angeles Fashion Week	Mid-October	Los Angeles

Useful knitwear terminology

A basic understanding of the various terms and visual examples associated with knitwear design is essential to show in your knitwear portfolio.

Warp and weft

Knits are created by the interlooping of yarns. The two main classifications are warp and weft knits.

Warp knits: These are made with yarns that zigzag back and forth, and run the length of the fabric to create columns (called wales), rather than a single row (called a course). They are almost always produced by machine because there is usually one yarn for each knitting needle. Common types of warp knits include tricot, Milanese knits, and raschel knits.

Weft knits: These are made with yarns that run horizontally from side to side across the width of the fabric. Horizontal courses build one on top of the other as the fabric is made, and in its simplest form a single yarn may be used. The fabric can be produced either flat like wovens or a tubular piece. The plain-knit stitch (jersey), the rib-knit stitch, and the purl stitch (which looks the same on both sides) are all weft knits.

Key construction terms

Cut and sew: Cut-and-sew garments are made with pre-knit yardage. Patterns are laid on top, cut, and then sewn in a similar way to woven fabrics.

Sweater knits: Sweater knits are made on special machines that knit the pattern pieces according to their intended shapes and are then assembled to form the garment.

Knit: The first basic stitch learned in knitting, which forms the front or right side of the work.

Purl: The second basic stitch learned, which forms the back or wrong side of the work.
These two stitches form plain knitting.

Key stitches, patterns, and techniques

Bobble: A 3-D effect created by multiplying stitches from a single stitch and then decreasing back down to the original stitch.

Cable: A twisted dimensional pattern that uses double-ended needles to create vine-like or geometric patterns.

Drop needle or needle out: An effect created by transferring one or more stitches onto the adjacent stitch, creating a ladder effect as the yarn is carried over the dropped stitch area on subsequent rows.

Engineered rib: A variety of rib stitches used in combination with one another to form the body of the knit garment.

Fair isle: A technique used to create multiple-colored patterns that are generally small in scale in comparison with intarsia knits. Fair isle knits are made by knitting the design into the pattern pieces at the same time, rather than assembling them like jigsaw-puzzle pieces. When a yarn color changes, a float is created on the wrong side and carried over to where the pattern resumes.

Float: The length of yarn carried over onto the back of the work when changing colors.

Full-fashioned: When stitches are transferred over to create shape at armholes, necklines, princess seams, etc.

Full needle rib: A machine double-bed rib that creates the effect of one-by-one rib on both sides of the garment.

Garter stitch: Every row is knit stitch, giving a reverse jersey look to both sides of the work.

Gauge: Term used to describe the size of yarn: 5gg, 7gg, 12gg, 16gg, and 24gg are most commonly used for machine sizes, and 3gg or 5gg are most commonly used for hand knits. Knitting a sample with your chosen yarn and measuring how many stitches equal one inch (2½ cm) and how many rows equal one inch (2½ cm) will enable you to map out your pattern. Note: Size of yarn thickness determines gauge.

Intarsia: A technique used to create multiple-colored patterns of any kind in knitwear. Shapes are generally large and are knit as separate pieces that are then fitted together to form the garment, rather like jigsaw-puzzle pieces.

Jacquard: A machine technique used to emulate intarsia patterns with a limited number of colors in repeat.

Jersey: Formed by knitting one row and purling one row.

Lace: Any amount of lace effects can be created with engineered pointelle patterns.

Marled: When two or more yarns of different color or size are knitted together to create a random pattern or texture. The pattern is visible on the back and front of the work.

Plaited: A machine technique used most often with Lurex or metallic yarn. One end of the novelty yarn is added along with the base yarn and is knitted only on the face of the work, so as not to create an itchy texture on the inside. (Has a similar look to marl.)

Pointelle: The effect created in the garment by knitting stitches together in one row and then adding the stitch back in the next knit row to create a hole.

Reverse jersey: A term for the reverse side of the work. This may be used as the front when a more textured look is preferred, and it often forms the background of cable patterns.

Rib: Made with alternate wales (vertical columns) of plain stitches and purl stitches on both sides of the fabric. Common structures are 1 x 1, 2 x 2, and so on.

Stockinette stitch: An old-fashioned term for jersey.

Variegated rib: An uneven combination of knit and purl (3 x 1, 5 x 3, and so on).

Basic trims and finishing techniques
Flat strapping: Full needle rib trim, used as facing, in side slits, or at necklines for a clean, finished look.

Linked: When a contrast trim is knitted separately and linked on after the garment is knitted. The stitches along

the edge are picked up and the trim is attached by a few rows of knit, which forms a seam inside the garment.

Picot: A decorative edge created by knitting regular pointelle holes along the middle of jersey trim and then folding the trim in half, so that the holes form an undulating edge.

Rib: Made with alternate wales (vertical columns) of plain stitches and purl stitches on both sides of the fabric. Common structures are 1 x 1, 2 x 2, and so on.

Self-start: Term used for a full-rib body where the rib itself forms the start and no additional trim is necessary. Sometimes a tighter tension is requested for ⅜ in. (1 cm) at the start to hold shape.

Single crochet: Stitches along edge are picked up and crocheted to give a simple finished edge.

Tubular: The most common finish used in machine knitting. Jersey is knitted twice the desired finished height, then folded and caught under on the inside to create a flat, clean, finished edge.

Index

Credits

Special thanks to Kelly Quinn for her remarkable work. I'm truly thankful!

Illustration and fashion design

Bessie Afnaim
Isaias O. Arias
Lizette Avineri
Leah Barton
Lauren Burnet
Virginia Burris
Anna Jayoon Choi
Hee Sung Choi
Ji Yoon Jennie Han
Kat Hoelck
Grace Hu
Seung Yeon Jee
Susan Kay
Paige Kettering
Diana Gayoung Kim
Sylvia Kwan
Hannah Learner
Kate Leaver
Jennifer Lee
Bo Bae Lee
Jin Hee Lee
Anna Hae Won Lee
Hee Lim
Yuen Chi Lo
Melissa Luning
Christine Mayes
Elif Muyesser
Paul Negron
Desiree Neman
Jessie Oh
Jon Pagels
Nancy Park
Myrtle Quillamor
John Paul Rangel
Jennifer Rubin
Silvia Santos
Sara Shahbazi
Laura Siegel
Nanae Takata
Tara La Tour
Hugo Tsang
Joseph Williams IV
Aiden Yoo
Clara Yoo

Photographers

Birsu Baseillar p62–63
Owen Bruce p104–105
Mike Devito: all illustration work
Maria Kavas p130
Jason Kim
Younghoon Kim p67
Benjemin Madav p26, 58, 60, 124
Ashley Minette p47
Georgia Nerheim p144–145
Grady O'Connor p1, 68
James Orlando p66
Federico Peltretti p69
Bill Durgin p149tl
David Schulze p148t,149tr

Quarto would also like to thank the following for supplying images:

l = left; r = right; t = top; b = bottom; c = center

UAL © Alys Tomlinson p9, 25tr, 57cr, 57br, 58, 60tl/bl, 61tr
OLSEN TWINS p14bl
DAN AND CORINA LECCA p14tr
Junky Styling www.junkystyling.co.uk Photo: Armando p15tl
Fashionstock p16bl/c/br
Rex Features p17tl/r, 89 all, 98, 104bl, 116
Getty Images p17br, 56, 104tr
SOOKIbaby is designed by Dijana Dotur. All designs and images are owned by Tiny Tribe Pty Ltd, an Australian owned and operated company. p106t/b
Jessica Stuart-Crump for Republik MTB p118
Jessica Stuart-Crump for Westbeach p119
Kitty Dong p123
Karen Millen p128, 139, 140, 141, 142

All other images are the copyright of Quarto Publishing plc. While every effort has been made to credit contributors, Quarto would like to apologize should there be any omissions or errors, and would be pleased to make the appropriate correction for future editions of the book.